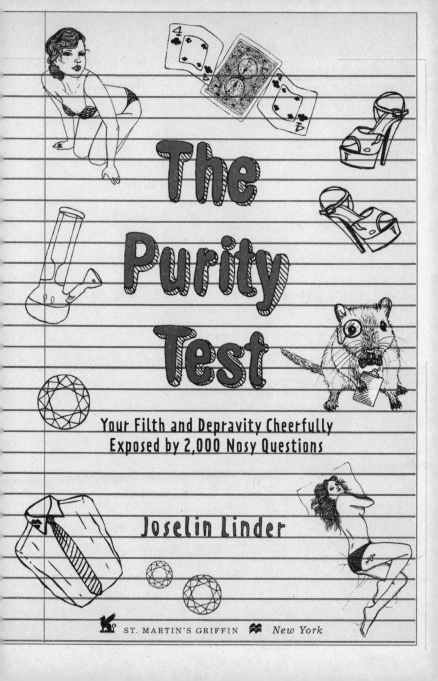

The Purity Test

Your Filth and Depravity Cheerfully Exposed by 2,000 Nosy Questions

Joselin Linder

ST. MARTIN'S GRIFFIN ❧ *New York*

Illustrations of Richard the Purity Gerbil © 2009
by Samantha Hahn

www.stmartins.com

Library of Congress Cataloging-in-Publication Data

Linder, Joselin.
    The purity test : your filth and depravity
cheerfully exposed by 2,000 nosy questions
Joselin Linder.—1st St. Martin's Griffin ed.
        p.   cm.
    ISBN-13: 978-0-312-38785-3
    ISBN-10: 0-312-38785-7
    1. Purity (Ethics)—Miscellanea.   2. Conduct of
life—Miscellanea.   I. Title.
  BJ1533.P97L56   2009
  170.28'7—dc22

                                        2008033591

        First Edition: February 2009

        10 9 8 7 6 5 4 3 2 1

For the twins,

you lovely, clean slates

Contents

Acknowledgments

I want to thank my great friend and agent-extra-ordinaire, Molly Lyons, for thinking of me when she hears good ideas and trying not to regret it even when I'm complaining. I'd like to thank both her and Joëlle Delbourgo and Associates for such remarkable support and council. I'd like to thank my editor, David Moldawer, for being the first to get excited about this book, and I don't mean "excited" like that. I'd also like to thank him for helping me organize everything clearly and skillfully. Also, thanks to Alyse Diamond for her supreme awesomeness.

I want to thank everyone I grilled over cocktails, beers, and (no) illegal drugs about what they enjoyed doing naked, alone, and in groups of two or more. I have to thank Eli Kirtz for his mathematical brilliance. I'd like to thank Brett of Facebook and John H. DuBois III of Armory.com for answering my "probing" questions. Also, thanks to Ryan, Alina, Sean M., Gabra, Sean-y G., Erica, Sari, Gabe, and all the others who tried out the test to make sure the questions were reasonable for real people and not just hookers and junkies. I want to thank in particular Kevin, Caroline, Karen, Philip, Wendy, Sam, Marni, and former members Abby and San for being the people that remind me every Tuesday at the Stoned Crow Writers Workshop why writing is the best thing ever. Tigers, this one's for you! (Too bad if you don't want it . . .)

I want to assure my mom and my sister that the knowledge procured for and prior to this book is not their fault and that I really, really love them. To my grandma, who is totally cool enough to read this book and continue to think I'm a good girl. I'd like to thank Aaron for his support, suggestions, and those last several pints of Guinness that took care of a few hundred questions. Also, thank you to our awesome dog, Dee Dee Ramone. Finally, I'd like to thank my father for not rolling over in his grave and understanding that I know a diatribe on methamphetamines is not necessarily what he meant when he instilled in me this great love of words.

The
Purity
Test

What Is Purity?

You probably think you picked this book up out of nostalgia. You might remember taking the Purity Test while eating s'mores around the fire during your last night at summer camp, or in the back of the gym with your classmates while you were supposed to be doing laps. But the real reason you're reading this is, deep down, you're still curious to see how your own little perversions rank with the rest of us. You want to know how *normal* you are.

It's a good question, one we first ask ourselves somewhere between November and February of fourth grade, as we begin to realize that certain things like teachers with high or low bulges make us feel . . . *funny*. Does everyone feel this way, we wonder. Or am I weird? Dirty? Impure?

How can we ever really, truly know?

Scientists, being scientists, measure purity with scientific accuracy. Let's say you have a sample of substance A, and you want to know how pure it is. You need to know how much of the sample is *really* substance A and how much is some other junk that got in there. The less other stuff, the greater the *purity* of your sample.

This book measures *your* purity in the same way. Substance A is you as your mommy made you, fresh from the womb: 100 percent pure. Then we'll measure how much of an impact the world has made on you over the years.

At this point, I'm sure you have a lot of questions. (Don't worry, I've got two thousand of them for you.) Judging purity, we have to deal with the mores of American society at the dawn of the twenty-first century. These rapidly shifting codes and beliefs make accuracy and objectivity difficult.

To give you a sense of the moral minefield we're about to stumble through together, here's a question: does being circumcised make you less pure?

On the one hand, circumcision is a change inflicted by the outside world. Like, *big time*. In terms of the scientific definition of purity, i.e. change from an original state, circumcision reduces purity.

However, scientists and the Bible pretty much agree that smegma (the funk that builds up beneath the hood of an uncircumcised penis) is impure. (To be fair, the Bible doesn't discuss smegma specifically, but it's there in the subtext.) Further, some men outgrow their foreskin at puberty, creating an unpleasant rubber band effect. These unfortunate men must endure the mohel's knife as adults.

Considering this, would it still be fair to call circumcision impure? No.

Another example: say you refuse medical treatment for a nasty infection because you're in a cult that denies the benefits of modern medicine. While one might argue that you remain pristine because no vaccination was administered, in reality you've become infested with a foreign bacteria that makes puss come out of your eyes. Is it safe to call your aversion to doctors impure? Yes.

So, things aren't entirely black and white, but this book doesn't pretend to be a perfect arbiter of truth.

Just kidding. This book is a perfect arbiter of truth.

Luckily, in most cases, the issue of purity is quite simple. Take sex. Sexual purity is fairly easy to measure. The less you've had, the more pure you remain. Whether sexual purity is something to be celebrated depends entirely on your belief system. In that sense, the Purity Test remains agnostic.

Manners and social standards serve a practical purpose, going all the way back to the early efforts of prehistoric humans learning to interact with one another without resorting to spears and rocks. Anthropologists tell us that social standards were explicitly laid out as early as the twenty-fourth century BCE. An Egyptian with too much time on his hands named Ptahhotep penned a list of the rules of civility, common behaviors passed down from ancestors who in turn had been trained by the gods. Much later, in the French courts of King Louis XIV the word "etiquette" first appeared referring to tickets inscribed with rules for proper behavior.

Stateside, George Washington wrote *Rules of Civility and Decent Behaviour in Company and Conversation* sometime before the age of sixteen (but sometime after the whole cherry tree incident). Rule #4 was truly ahead of its time: "In the Presence of Others Sing not to yourself with a humming Noise, nor Drum with your Fingers or Feet."

Papa Washington covered quite a bit in this early literary effort, but he never mentioned whether or not it was improper to blow yourself. So, is it?

Rules of Civility and Decent Behaviour in Company and Conversation (highlights) by George Washington

- Shew Nothing to your Friend that may affright him.
- Gaze not on the marks or blemishes of Others and ask not how they came. . . .
- Speak not in an unknown Tongue in Company but in your own Language . . .
- Think before you Speak . . .
- Rince not your Mouth in the Presence of Others.
- Let your Recreations be Manfull not Sinfull.
- Labour to keep alive in your Breast that Little Spark of Celestial fire Called Conscience.

Yes.

Purity is relative. We are all clean slates when we enter the world. What we are *allowed* to do and not do fluctuates over time and across cultural divides. Someone raised in New Delhi will follow a different set of rules for purity than a kid in Arkansas. But even within Arkansas, the rules can change from house to house. Where one set of parents might feel comfortable discussing the parts of the body and their functions with their kids, parents at the house next door might prefer to leave it to the experts—other kids on the playground and MTV. For some, purity is keeping private things private: skin covered, mouths clean. For others, purity means not taking a crap with the stall door open.

As the world shrinks, it becomes clearer and clearer that one person's freakish perversion is another's harmless diversion.

The Forefather of the Purity Test

In 1948, biologist Alfred Kinsey published *Sexual Behavior in the Human Male,* a groundbreaking report on male sexuality. Overnight, a professor of entomology obsessed with fruit flies became a celebrity, and his stature only grew in 1953 when he published a second report, *Sexual Behavior in the Human Female.*

That World War II ended and this once-taboo topic became fodder for everyday discussion at almost the same time isn't surprising. More than one hundred million people had been mobilized for war in Europe alone. Eighteen-year-old boys were blown to bits. Civilians were systematically murdered en masse. Women left home for the workforce. Humankind's innocence was collectively shattered. Everyone retreated to their corners to lick their wounds. A universal effort to find meaning in the midst of postwar existential angst began.

"How do we feel less alone?" we wondered. The answer was simple: find out what everyone else is doing behind closed doors!

Sigmund Freud and his cohorts had already given birth to psychoanalysis. Suddenly the "why" of human behavior took a backseat to the "what." After all, how can you discuss *why* we do things if we still don't know what we actually *do*?

Enter the Kinsey Reports. Through anonymous surveys, Kinsey collected information not just on what people did in the sack, but also on what they wanted to be doing. Thanks to the Reports, a picture of American sexuality began to emerge. More importantly, a dialogue had begun.

Social boundaries change over time, but they don't always loosen. The sexual liberation of the twenties was long gone by the socially conservative fifties. The widening use of contraceptives in the sixties gave birth to the sexual revolution (which gave birth to, well, not much, thanks to contraceptives), which the AIDS epidemic subsequently squashed in the eighties.

But through the cycles of prurience and prudishness, thanks to the impact of the Kinsey Reports we can find

A Few Nuggets from the Kinsey Report

92% of males and 62% of females masturbate

68% of males and 50% of females engaged in premarital sex

37% of males and 13% of females had instances of at least one homosexual experience that resulted in orgasm

the idea of bestiality horrifying but still acknowledge its existence. Thanks to one sex-obsessed researcher, we can finally ask the question, "Have you ever applied any gels, liquids, or creams to someone else's asshole for either sexual or medicinal purposes?" and get an answer. Thus, Alfred Kinsey should rightly be considered the forefather of the Purity Test in all its glory.

A Brief History of Purity Tests

What is the Purity Test, and where did it come from? In its most recent incarnation, the test consists of a series of yes-or-no questions producing a score in the form of a percentage. This percentage or "Purity Number" indicates the damage the test taker has incurred to his or her moral, spiritual, and physical purity. The Purity Number is in direct proportion to the number of *no* answers. For example, on a one-hundred-question Purity Test, if someone answers *no* forty times, their Purity Number will be 40 percent.

The rank-and-file of Purity Test historians disagree on this point, but given the raging fascination humans have with nosing around in one another's business, it's likely that some form of the Purity Test existed in written form since the invention of hieroglyphs, or at least since the invention of the so-called "hummer" blowjob, which came less than a century later. (The origins and provenance of the oral Purity Test tradition are beyond the scope of this book.)

Thanks to the wide availability of typewriters and mimeograph machines, Purity Tests proliferated at schools and summer camps across the United States in the seventies and eighties, but this form of distribution was slow and unreliable, and the tests themselves were prone to confiscation by parents, teachers, and members of the clergy. For the Purity Test to truly take hold as a youth phenomenon, a new form of distribution was required. Enter the Internet, a worldwide network of computers created single-handedly by former Vice President Al Gore.

Around 1980, the occupants of Baker House, a dorm

at the Massachusetts Institute of Technology, developed the Unisex Purity Test, one of the first Internet-distributed Purity Tests. Despite its misleading name, the test consisted of two separate sections of a hundred questions, one for each of the two genders recognized at the time. Later in the eighties, test makers and the tests themselves became harder for the dedicated Purity Test historian to track. The breakneck speed at which personal computers and the Internet spread from universities into businesses and homes only slightly outpaced the spread of the Purity Test, which found its way from modem to modem, dial-up bulletin board to dial-up bulletin board.

The early Internet was a powerful tool, but it was still complicated and difficult for the average person to use, which kept the Purity Test from truly entering the mainstream. In 1989 John H. DuBois III, a Santa Cruz–based Internet expert, or "geek," wrote a program allowing the Purity Test to be taken and scored on a personal computer using a new language called HTML. In 1994, after Tim Berners-Lee gave the gift of the World Wide Web to mankind, DuBois uploaded the first Web-based Purity Test.

No longer would test takers have to waste paper and risk discovery by printing thousands of questions on primitive dot-matrix printers and then carefully shred page after page of the completed tests. Now, anyone with an Internet connection could take a Purity Test and receive a score automatically from the comfort and privacy of their own Web browser.

By 1999, the tests on DuBois's Web site peaked in their popularity, with around three million tests submitted for scoring. The number has since tapered to about one million per year, mostly because so many other Web sites feature alternative versions.

Purity Tests are now of interest to a whole new wave of researchers of human behavior. Not to mention the one hundred thousand people who have taken the Official 100 Question Sexual Purity Test on Facebook, located at apps.facebook.com/hundredpurity/. Its author, Bret, explained the appeal of the Purity Test as follows: "Cool people tend to be cool because they have done cool things. These tests are how coolness can be ranked. Or how people can figure out how to get cooler."

Bret's first experience with a Purity Test came during his freshman year in college. A sophomore girl handed one out to a room full of freshmen. While taking the test, Bret, still innocent and naïve, noticed a pretty girl at his side check off that she had slept with two members of the same family and that those two members were a father and son. "I never looked at that girl the same way again!"

People are better defined by their actions than their words. We are what we do. For instance, is it even possible to more succinctly describe the personality of Bret's former roommate than to relate the fact that he once drank vodka through his asshole? This act, which resulted in inebriation without unnecessary calories, speaks volumes to the young man's character in a way that his words never could.

There is so much we don't know about one another. And so much we wish to understand about ourselves. The Purity Test is a way to settle up with the universe, to look at the best and worst of our own true natures in the clear light of day. The test offers an unparalleled opportunity to judge, categorize, and rank ourselves, and—finally—discover our own true place in the cosmos.

"A test?" you ask. "Really? A test can do all that?"

Well, no. But whether you're the kind of person who avoids handshakes for fear of accidental pregnancy, or enjoys mud-wrestling your sister in the nude in front of the neighbors' children, the test won't make things any worse.

A Sample of Purity Tests on the Web

Feminist's Purity Test

www.geocities.com/SoHo/Coffeehouse/2706/puritytest.html

The Rocky Horror Purity Test

www.rockymusic.org/purity.php

The Queen Purity Test

www.lagmonster.info/games/purity/queen.html

The Greedy Bisexual Purity Test

www.armory.com/tests/greedy_bisexual.html

Preparing to Take the Purity Test

These tests are for your entertainment and should be approached as such. In other words, put on your "I'm having fun!" shoes and wipe that puss off. Share it with friends, but maybe not with people you want to mother or father your children—and it goes without saying that you shouldn't share it with your mother or father.

Before you try any of the things you read about in

these pages, consult our handy reference guide at the back of the book. We support dirty minds, but not things like passing on STDs or accidentally hanging yourself from the clothing rod in the closet while practicing autoerotic asphyxiation. And we are completely opposed to hurting anything that has nerve endings— even if they are furry and unable to testify in court. If it can't or won't consent, DON'T TOUCH IT!

Now stretch.

The Purity Test

Welcome to the Purity Test!

Here you will find, across five different tests, two thousand questions to determine your moral, spiritual, ethical, and physical purity. The first is a Basic Purity Test. Use it as a warm-up. This hundred-question test is designed to give you a quick guesstimate of your purity or lack thereof. It will not go into nuanced detail but it will crack the door open on the hazardous wasteland of your depravity.

Next you will find the General Purity Test, a sixteen-hundred-question behemoth. It'll take substantially longer to complete, but in return for your effort you will ultimately receive a deeper, harder, more satisfying result. (As well as ideas on how to enhance your Purity Number in entirely new ways.)

Still, in this crazy world, it's entirely possible that some of you will tear right through the BPT and the GPT and remain unsatisfied. "More!" you will bellow. "These tests did not speak to *me*!" Then what?

First, there is the Male Purity Test. This test contains one hundred questions designed specifically for the perverse minds of straight men and lumberjacks of all persuasions. The Female Purity Test is for the woman who has everything, including a stubborn yeast infection. This test is also appropriate for a woman trapped in a man's body, or a man seeking his inner slut. This hundred-question test should tell you once and for all what it means to be a girl who can't get enough or who doesn't want any more ever again.

The Gay Purity Test is geared mostly toward gay guys, and though it touches on lesbians and bis, it pretty much mills around such pastimes as sucking cock at the gym and fucking boys who swear that for fifty bucks they are or will be "of age." Tread lightly into this incredibly gay (in every way) Purity Test.

A few rules apply to each and every test. Don't worry, a reminder will, um, remind you, before each individual test for those of you too fried to remember what was just said. (Huh?)

First, for the sake of simplicity, or perhaps to confuse the hell out of you, this book would like to offer you an "Or Something Similar" clause. You may invoke this clause anytime you see a question pertaining to an act that you believe you were very close to completing, or that you did in fact complete, just not exactly as it is presented in the question. In other words, if a question asks, "Have you ever secretly watched your cousin undressing for a shower?" and you think you haven't watched her undress for a shower but you have done *something similar*, like watch her undress to change into her soccer uniform, you can score that point as a yes.

If you'd prefer to take each question at it's most literal, this probably means you are a big dork or vaguely OCD, but you have my blessing and are free to do so.

Your Purity Number can be obtained in as few as 100 questions or in as many as 2,000: Add up your *no* answers.

- If you answer 100 questions, your score is exactly the number of *no* answers you total.
- If you answer 200 questions, your score is the number of *no* answers divided by 2.

- If you answer 300 questions, your score is the number of *no* answers divided by 3.
- 400 questions, divide *no* answers by 4.
- 500, divide by 5.
- 600, divide by 6.
- 700, by 7.
- 800, by 8.

Do you see where we're going with this?

- 900, divide by 9.
- 1,000, divide by 10.
- Etc.

At 1,900, what do you think you do? Go ahead and guess. Yes. Divide by 19.

And at last when you reach 2,000 questions, add up all of your *no* answers, crack open a Heineken, and divide by (let's hear it folks!) 20.

To get a true Purity Number, call the number a percent. In other words, 560 *no* answers out of 700 questions, divided by 7 equals 80. Therefore, your Purity Number is 80 percent.

After dividing the number, you might find yourself

burdened with a remainder or a decimal. What do you do? After you grab your hair in your fisted palms and scream really loudly, drop those numbers (72.8=72 percent) or round them up or down depending on your mood (72.8 rounded up is 73 percent, rounded down is 72 percent), and then get over it.

Again, to you all, welcome to the Purity Test. Don't trip over the dead animals or bloody maxi pads on your way in.

The Basic Purity Test

The Basic Purity Test won't hold your hand, give you head, or get you out alive. It won't provide you with a Purity Number accurate to five decimal places. But it will give you new insights into yourself and offer a starting point from which to pull it the fuck together.

Scoring:

- Answer all one hundred questions.
- For each *no* add one point.
- Your total *no* answers is your Purity Number.
- Write this number as a percentage.

Richard the Purity Gerbil says:

Hi. I'm Richard. Now don't freak out. I'm not a rat. I'm a gerbil. Richard the Purity Gerbil! Gerbils are good at maneuvering into tight spots, so I'm going to help you work your way into each test.

Let's start with the Basic Purity Test. It is made up of one hundred questions of deplorable depravity and downright dangerous degradation. I'd say it's right up your alley, but I don't know you yet. After you take this sucker, though, whole 'nother story. You will be as transparent as a cracked-out runner going full tilt on a hamster wheel. Just saying.

Here are the rules:

If you come across a question such as "Have you ever

1. Have you ever kissed anyone on the first date?
2. Have you ever read someone else's diary without their permission?
3. Have you ever played Twister in mixed company?
4. How about naked?
5. Have you ever dated more than one person at

had a threesome on a sailboat heading for open sea?" and you think, "Huh. Almost. I've been in a foursome on a sailboat heading for one of the Great Lakes!" or something similar, you can give yourself a *yes* based on the "Or Something Similar" clause.

Scores for this section are as easy to obtain as a "seeing to" in a prison yard with your pants down:

- Answer *yes* or *no.*
- Keep track of your *no* answers
- The total *no* answers is your Purity Number.
- *Example: If you say* no *75 times, you are 75% pure.*

Now go have fun.

a time without one or both of them knowing about the other?

6. Have you ever dated more than one person at a time and both of them knew about the other?

7. Have you ever openly praised someone's sexual style?

8. Have you ever had an AIDS test?

9. Have you ever bathed or showered with anyone?

10. Have you ever dry humped against anyone?

11. Have you ever cursed in front of your parents or grandparents?

12. Have you ever shaved off your pubic hair?

13. Have you ever worn your lover's undergarments?

14. Have you ever asked a very tall person how the weather is up there, or a bald person if they wax their head, or something similar?

15. Has anyone ever watched you masturbate?

16. Have you ever watched anyone else masturbate?

17. Have you ever used over-the-counter sleeping pills?

18. Or taken NoDoz or ephedrine to stay awake?

19. Have you ever faked an injury to get drugs?

20. Ever injured yourself to get them?

21. Have you ever watched a porn with people of both sexes present?

22. Do you know what your parents' fetishes are?

23. Do they know yours?

24. When you see an animal in heat or a dog humping does it turn you on a little or freak you out a little?

25. Have you ever drawn a pentagram on a wall?

26. Ever doodled swastikas or confederate flags?

27. Have you ever put a hole through a wall in a fit of rage and then failed to ever repair it?

28. Have you ever pulled a fire alarm and evacuated a building?

29. Have you ever spent more than five consecutive hours online?

30. More than ten?

31. Have you ever spent the night in a line waiting for tickets to anything?

32. Have you ever slept through an entire class?

33. Ever woken yourself up with your own snores in a movie theater?

34. Have you ever called either of your parents a swear word?

35. Have you ever shown up to work in mismatched socks?

36. Have you ever gotten into an elevator in a high-rise building and pushed all the buttons then yelled, "Shit, I forgot something!" and ran off, leaving the other suckers on the elevator to enjoy the ride?

37. Have you ever waxed your back, ass, or upper lip?

38. Have you ever slept with anyone on your first date?

39. Have you ever raised an animal from birth (like a chicken or a pig) then slaughtered and eaten it?

40. Have you ever smoked pot rolled into Bible pages?

41. Do your parents probably love the family dog more than they love you?

42. Have you ever walked around a public place in the nude?

43. Have you ever had sex in more than three positions in one session?

44. Have you ever had sex without using birth control?

45. Have you ever thought you might have an STD?

46. Did you have one?

47. Have you ever had sex with someone from a foreign country?

48. Have you ever had sex with someone who was married?

49. Ever had sex with someone other than your spouse when you were married?

50. Have you ever had scratches left on your body after sex?

51. Ever left scratches?

52. Have you ever made someone gay turn bi?

53. Have you had sex with more than twenty people (over the span of your life)?

54. Have you ever had sex with more than one person in twenty-four hours?

55. Have you ever seen a snuff film or watched someone truly die on film?

56. Have you ever made out a check you knew would bounce?

57. Have you ever urinated on anyone intentionally?

58. Ever allowed anyone to pee on you?

59. Ever been in a food fight?

60. Ever stored your own shit in a freezer?

61. Have you ever taken valium?

62. Have you ever sold any of your possessions to get drugs?

63. Have you ever tried to plan an orgasm at the peak of a nitrous rush?

64. Have you ever had sex while drunk?

65. Had sex while high on pot?

66. Had sex while tripping?

67. Had sex while on coke?

68. Have you ever forgone an orgasm because you were too drunk to get there?

69. Have you ever been in an orgy?

70. Have you ever participated in a game where everyone takes either a drug or a placebo and you don't know who got what until the drug takes effect?

71. Ever done 69?

72. Ever been in a 69-circle?

73. Have you ever watched a porn with yours or someone else's parents?

74. Have you ever used a doll of any kind for purposes of masturbation?

75. Does the idea of fucking a robot turn you on?

76. Have you ever masturbated with a mannequin or to thoughts of one?

77. Ever sniffed dirty underpants that belonged to someone other than you?

78. Ever sniffed anyone's underpants (yours included) and found yourself horrified?

79. Turned on?

80. Have you ever taken underpants from someone you'd had sex with as a memento?

81. Ever had sex on a trampoline?

82. Ever had it in a phone booth?

83. A voting booth?

84. A dressing room?

85. Have you ever been to a museum of torture?

86. How about a sex museum?

87. Have you ever gone to an AA meeting just to watch the drunks get lame and weepy?

88. Ever gone because you were one of the drunks?

89. Have you ever gone to an AA meeting drunk?

90. Have you ever consumed alcohol that had been poured through someone's ass crack and into a cup?

91. Have you ever eaten something so spicy it made you sweat or cry?

92. Ever prepared a meal that began with a live animal you were going to have to cook (insects and shellfish included)?

93. Ever eaten something that was still alive when you took your first bite?

94. Have you ever consciously used meat stock or other meat by-product in an otherwise vegetarian dish and then swore it had no meat in it to a vegetarian who came over for dinner?

95. Have you ever nicknamed your partner's sex parts?

96. Have you ever shot and killed an animal for sport?

97. Have you ever laughed at the pain and suffering of your fellow man?

98. Have you ever written a Purity Test?

99. Have you ever spent more than an hour answering Purity Test questions?

100. Ever contemplated why?

YOUR BASIC PURITY NUMBER:
_____%

The General Purity Test

N ow you're ready for the big guns. Don't worry if you don't have all day, no one's timing you. But, to know your worth as a human being to the point where you'll be correcting Saint Peter's notes on yourself at the pearly gates, toss back a couple of cans of Red Bull and do the whole test right now!

About the Test

The test is broken into four sections:

The Purity Test

Sexual Purity—400 Questions

Your Sexual Purity reflects what kind of slut you are: a little slut, or an enormous one. These four hundred questions will help determine how much therapy (and how many antibiotics) you'll need, and no, that doesn't mean naked-with-a-hot-sex-therapist-therapy either! This section will give you a dangerously accurate reading of your scabies risks as well as what kind of hooker you would make—and maybe even how much money you could earn!

Drug Purity—400 Questions

If you manage to hork enough Ritalin to sit through these four hundred questions, the drug purity section will tell you whether you need a Life Flight to the nearest rehab facility, a bus ticket away from your peer group, or a joint.

Criminal Behavior Purity—400 Questions

If your felonious imagination can scheme it, it's in this section of the test. The criminal behavior section will point you to the nearest squad car to turn yourself in (or to toss eggs at). But don't leave your answers lying around, in case the 5-O comes by.

Cardinal Vice Purity—400 Questions

Cardinal purity measures the extent to which you've violated each of the cardinal (a.k.a. seven deadly) sins. If you hear thunder in the distance while completing this section, duck and cover because you're about to be on the receiving end of some holy vengeance.

Scoring

To generate a Purity Number, keep track of your *no* answers either mentally or on paper—like the way you've recorded the history of your drug use on your body with those premature wrinkles, distended belly, and track marks.

If you answer 100 questions, the total number of *no* answers you have is your Purity Number when stated as a percent.

In other words, 86 no *answers gives you a Purity Number of 86 percent.*

For each subsequent set of 100 questions, generate a Purity Number by *dividing,* the way a crack whore is *divided* from her kids by Children's Services.

In other words, if you answer 200 questions, total your *no* answers and divide by two.

120 no answers divided by 2 makes the Purity Number 60 percent.

If you answer 300 questions, total your *no* answers and divide by three.

240 no answers makes someone 80 percent pure.

Continuing in this vein (like a needle full of dope), if you answer 1,000 questions, divide by ten, 1600 questions, divide by sixteen.

By this token, for 2,000 *no* answers totaled, divide by 20.

If at any point you find yourself confronted with a remainder or a decimal point, go ahead and drop it like a bad coke habit, or round it up like the bitchin' curves of a cherry red ZR1. If you answer 1,200 questions and total 1,023 *no* answers, divide by twelve.

The number 85.25 makes a Purity Number of 85 percent.

If you follow these instructions, you can bet your bottom bong hit that your score will be more pure than garden-grown chronic from your own backyard.

The Sexual
Purity Test

America was settled by Europeans fleeing more than just religious persecution: Europe was a filthy place back then, and not just in terms of rats and plagues. We're talking raunchy theater, dirty limericks, and a general appetite for all things heathen. The pilgrims crossed the Atlantic to found a new, G-rated homeland (where G stands for Godly).

Luckily, America's native populations weren't such anal douche bags about covering up their jiggly bits and denying all human passions. For instance, the Huron people weren't limited to one sexual partner for life. If a woman grew tired of her partner, she simply asked him to leave. For many tribes, sex and marriage were often the norm, but there was still a deep reverence for earthly pleasures. No wonder the settlers were jealous! Forget land—the Native Americans' real natural resource was a swinging lifestyle.

Sexual hypocrisy is one of the cornerstones of the USA. In the twenties, despite a prudish Victorian façade, speakeasies and brothels thrived. In fact, people were having so much sex they failed to see the economy heading toward a cliff. During the Great Depression, while sex certainly provided an escape from the misery of the Dust Bowl, people were understandably more interested in the buns you could eat.

Veterans of the Second World War returned from Europe and Japan looking for stability, and they got it. Everyone was so sexually repressed in the fifties that married characters on sitcoms had separate beds. Luckily, the emergence of the Pill in the sixties sparked a sexual revolution—that crashed and burned thanks to HIV in the eighties.

Today, condoms and dental dams in hand, we've begun to rediscover the joys of a little afternoon delight or a tawdry one-night stand. Some of us relish this return to our fun and filthy ways. Others are trying their best to rock the boat back the other way.

A recent study compared sexuality in different countries. For those of you who are interested in sexual purity compared at a global level, the following is a list of the study's highlights organized by number. For the rest of you, perhaps this will help you organize future vacation plans:

- 11: The number of minutes on average people in Thailand spend on foreplay.
- 12: The average number of sex partners in Iceland.
- 15: The average age at which Germans and Icelanders lose their virginity.

Richard the Purity Gerbil says:

Here you are at the section that covers, or uncovers, sexual purity, a fact that is probably making you all sweaty and ticklish, you freakin' perv. Sexual purity is an exploration of cavities you've filled, would like to fill, or can't wait to fill again, and I'm not just saying that as your friendly neighborhood gerbil. (Wink, wink.)

Similar rules apply to this test as are applied to all of the other tests. For example, if you come across a question like "Have you ever done the dirty deed with a chicken in a barn?" and you think, "I fucked a chicken, but not in a barn. It was in a school basement!" or something similar, you can give yourself a *yes* based on the "Or Something Similar" clause.

- 22: The average number of minutes folks in the U.K. spend on foreplay.
- 38: The percentage of people in India who will watch porn with a partner.
- 46: The number of times on average per year the Japanese make time for sex. (However, what they lack in quantity they make up for in some remarkable kinks and fetishes.)
- 61: The percentage of the Italian population enjoying orgasms.

Scores for this section are as easy to obtain as a blowjob through a glory hole:

- Keep track of your *no* answers.
- Divide your total after 400 questions by 4.
- Drop any decimals or remainders.
- Add a percentage.
- *Example: 290* no *answers divided by 4 is 72.5, which makes your Purity Number 72 percent.*

Ta da!

If you need me again I'll be burrowed deeply in a dark, damp place, quivering with expectation!

- 80: The percentage of people watching porn with their partners in Croatia.
- 137: The average number of times per year French people have sex. (Are you still calling them Freedom Fries? I don't think so. . . .)

Where is the USA in all of this? Our great nation rarely topped any lists or fell into their bottoms. This may come as no surprise. After all, we are a nation founded by religious fundamentalists with a revulsion to all things sexual, and yet somehow became the birthplace of a subculture called Furry Fandom consisting of those aroused by anthropomorphic animals like Bugs Bunny. So average sounds about right.

We can all hope for a day when the world won't need a sexual Purity Test, when fucking and fingering will be considered as natural as a church picnic on a sunny afternoon. But until that time, our sexual purity will continue to be measured. So at the very least we can take charge of our destinies, and do the measuring ourselves.

1. Have you ever held the hand of someone you were dating in public?
2. As an adult, have you ever held hands with an adult of the same sex in public?

3. Did you ever try to kiss someone and get rejected?

4. Have you ever kissed your own reflection in a mirror?

5. Have you ever made out with a pillow?

6. Have you ever made out with a doll?

7. Did you have your first French kiss before high school?

8. Did you ever get your braces locked into someone else's?

9. Did you ever fantasize, in detail, about kissing someone you didn't know?

10. Have you ever French kissed anyone of the opposite sex?

11. Have you ever wished you were kissing someone while in the middle of kissing someone else?

12. Did you have your first French kiss just to get it out of the way instead of really wanting it?

13. Have you ever made out with a person during a play (like *Romeo and Juliet*)?

14. Have you ever walked in on someone watching porn and decided to sit down and watch some of it with them?

15. Have you ever been completely grossed out by a hetero porno?

16. Have you ever watched a complete porn movie from beginning to end?

17. Have you ever masturbated while watching a porn movie?

18. Do you read a weekly sex column?

19. Have you ever brought yourself to orgasm with your clothes on in private?

20. Did you ever reject someone trying to kiss you?

21. Have you ever kissed someone of the same sex as you?

22. Have you ever masturbated while at work or in school?

23. Have you ever had a sex fantasy about a relative?

24. Have you ever had an orgasm in a dream?

25. Have you ever had an orgasm while you were awake?

26. Have you ever been kissed in such a way that you found yourself really turned on?

27. Do TV wrestling shows or other shows where people fight turn you on? (Be honest!)

28. Did you ever masturbate to a cartoon? (And yes, Bugs Bunny is included.)

29. Have you ever found any of the Smurfs attractive?

30. Have you ever been completely turned on during a math class at school?

31. Have you ever used a body part other than genitalia to simulate oral sex? (Sucking on a finger or toe or licking a mouth in a specific way all count!)

32. Have you ever danced seductively by yourself?

33. Have you ever danced seductively in public fully aware that you were being watched and liked it?

34. Have you ever grinded on the dance floor with someone of the same sex as you?

35. Did you ever take your clothes off in front of someone you were or hoped to be intimate with?

36. Have you ever licked someone's armpit?

37. Did you have sex for the first time to get it out of the way instead of because you really wanted it?

38. Have you ever wished you could make out with your teacher?

39. Have you ever gone home with a stranger from a bar?

40. Have you ever taken a stranger home from a bar?

41. Do you enjoy listening to the sexual exploits of your friends more often than not?

42. Have you ever danced naked in front of a mirror and enjoyed watching yourself?

43. Have you ever told a dirty joke?

44. Have you ever written down a dirty fantasy?

45. Have you ever had a fantasy about a friend of one of your parents?

46. Have you ever flirted fully consciously with a married person?

47. Have you ever flirted shamelessly with a teacher or professor even though you didn't necessarily find them attractive?

48. Have you ever found any of your doctors attractive?

49. Have you ever fantasized about sex with your doctor?

50. Do you ever think about being kissed by your therapist or a therapist in general?

51. Have you ever made out with your significant other in public?

52. Did you ever try to guess how big someone's penis was by the bulge in their pants?

53. Have you ever thought a girl's boobs were one size until you got her bra off and realized the hardware had you tricked?

54. Have you ever made out in a car?

55. Did you ever walk in on your parents having sex?

56. Have either of your parents ever walked in on you masturbating?

57. Have you ever gone out on a date with someone of a different race or religion out of curiosity?

58. Did you ever turn someone on by blowing in their ear or on their neck? In other words, without touching them below the neck?

59. Have you ever given a butt massage?

60. Have you ever received a butt massage?

61. Have you ever licked someone's already licked ice cream cone?

62. Have you ever studied your naked body in a mirror?

63. Have you ever "touched tongues" with someone of the same sex before the age of ten?

64. Have you ever "touched tongues" with an immediate family member?

65. Have you ever chewed someone else's gum?

66. Have you ever had a close, intimate inspection of someone else's genitals?

67. Did you ever play the game, "If you show me, I'll show you?" before you hit puberty?

68. How about after?

69. Have you ever acted out a soap opera or movie you'd seen with your siblings, including kissing?

70. Have you ever put a book between your face and the face of someone else and made out with it, pretending to make out with each other?

71. Have you ever had phone sex?

72. Ever had IM sex?

73. Have you ever had sex in the missionary position?

74. Have you ever used lingerie to turn each other on?

75. Did you ever jerk off or rub one out on your partner?

76. Have you ever gone from violently fighting to passionately kissing without a break in between?

77. Have you ever masturbated while looking at your stepmom while she's outside sunbathing?

78. Have you ever made out with a step-sibling?

79. Have you ever gone out with someone else's boyfriend or girlfriend that you'd been attracted to without that person's knowledge, even if you and the boyfriend/girlfriend agreed it was just a platonic outing?

80. Have you ever been in or watched a wet T-shirt contest?

81. Have you ever had someone lick your spine from bottom to top?

82. Have you ever left a hickey on someone's neck?

83. Have you ever left a hickey on someone's neck on purpose?

84. Have you ever given oral sex?

85. Have you ever had an orgasm through oral sex?

86. Have you ever had your butt hole licked?

87. Did you ever French kiss your cousin?

88. Have you ever cleaned someone's belly button out with your tongue?

89. Have you ever had whipped cream eaten off of you?

90. Have you ever fingered anyone?

91. Have you ever licked your own or someone else's finger after fingering someone?

92. Did you ever kiss anyone during a game (like Truth or Dare)?

93. Have you ever asked someone you were making out with to leave the room so you could masturbate?

94. Or have you ever slipped into the bathroom to masturbate after a make-out session?

95. Have you ever had lipstick left on your private parts?

96. Have you ever engaged in sexual intercourse?

97. Have you ever encouraged your partner with a phrase like, "Fuck me!" while engaging in sexual intercourse?

98. Have you ever called out to God while in the throes of an orgasm?

99. Have you ever told your partner the plotline to a porn in order to arouse them?

100. Have you ever licked someone's teeth, both top and bottom?

101. At your first French kiss, did you make the first move? (If it was a mutual initiation, then answer "yes.")

102. Have you ever been rejected trying to put your hand in someone's pants?

103. Have you ever rejected someone trying to put their hand down your pants?

104. Have you ever been felt up by someone of the same sex?

105. Have you ever tasted someone else's semen?

106. How about your own? (Ladies get a free "no" on this one . . .)

107. Do you like the taste of semen?

108. Have you ever tasted someone else's pussy?

109. Would you say you liked the taste of pussy?

110. Have you ever tasted your own pussy? (Men get a free "no" on this one if they want it . . .)

111. Have you ever looked down at your own body when you were naked?

112. Ever used a vibrator by yourself?

113. Have you ever gone to a sex therapist with a partner?

114. Have you ever had oral sex with a platonic friend just out of curiosity?

115. Have you ever had pity sex with anyone?

116. Have you ever had sex with a cat on the bed?

117. How about a dog?

118. Ever had a child under the age of one in the room during sex?

119. Did you have sex before the age of twenty for the first time?

120. Did you ever have sex with a fraternity brother or sorority sister?

121. Have you ever given or received a blowjob *after* you had already had sexual intercourse?

122. In the course of your sexual development, did you have sexual intercourse *before* oral sex?

123. Have you ever had sex underwater?

124. Have you ever had sex while watching yourself in a mirror?

125. Have you ever been paid to have sex with anyone?

126. Have you ever paid for sex?

127. Have you ever had sex at a rock concert?

128. Ever had to run away from someone trying to fuck you?

129. Ever swam from someone trying to touch you with their privates?

130. Ever been chased by someone trying to take your clothes off?

131. Ever lied to get out of fucking someone?

132. Have you ever had breakup sex?

133. Have you ever had sex while you were really pissed off at the person you were having sex with?

134. Have you ever vomited while giving oral sex?

135. Did you ever fantasize, in detail, about fucking someone you didn't know?

136. Have you ever forgotten a sex partner's name while you were having intimate relations?

137. Have you ever had sex in a public area of a bar or club?

138. Have your ever masturbated in public?

139. Have you ever masturbated by humping against a pillow?

140. Did you ever use a vibrator to masturbate with?

141. Have you ever given or received oral sex on an airplane?

142. How about while driving a car?

143. Have you ever claimed to be allergic to sex fluids to get out of performing oral sex?

144. Does a hairy back/ass on a man or hairy armpits/legs on a woman turn you on?

145. Have you ever been handcuffed or tied up during an intimate moment?

146. Have you ever tied someone up and had sex with them?

147. Ever had sex blindfolded?

148. Have you ever been mistaken for a homosexual (if you are hetero)?

149. Ever been mistaken for a homosexual (if you are hetero) and enjoyed it?

150. Have you ever taken a bite of someone else's food after they have bitten into it?

151. Does the idea of sex with a dwarf turn you on?

152. How about sex with a giant?

153. Have you ever had sex with a person of a different race?

154. Have you ever had oral sex at work?

155. Have you ever knowingly made out with a second cousin or distant relative?

156. Have you ever masturbated with a stuffed animal?

157. Do you like thinking about same-sex sex? (No matter which sex you prefer to actually fuck.)

158. Can you look at a nontraditionally sexy body part (like a toe, foot, or wrist) and feel yourself get hot?

159. Have you ever participated in a circle-jerk or something similar?

160. Have you ever participated in a threesome where you were the only person of your sex in the group?

161. Have you ever gone along with sex even though you didn't really feel like having it?

162. Have you ever given a lap-dance in private to a lover?

163. Have you ever kissed a teacher in a sexual way?

164. Have you ever had sexual intercourse on an airplane?

165. Have you ever slept with someone more than ten years older than you?

166. Have you ever slept with someone more than ten years younger than you?

167. Have you ever had sexual relations with a stranger at a bar? (In the bathroom of the bar is still "at a bar.")

168. Have you ever made out with your first cousin?

169. Have you ever driven off at the wrong exit to follow a hottie in another car?

170. Do you sometimes think oral sex is disgusting but have it anyway?

171. Have you ever gagged while performing oral sex?

172. Have you ever had someone else's finger inside your asshole?

173. How about your own finger?

174. Have you ever received oral sex and not reciprocated for any reason even though it was clear it was expected of you?

175. Have you ever had anal sex?

176. Have you ever swallowed semen?

177. Have you ever rented a porn movie?

178. Have you ever watched gay porn and enjoyed it?

179. Do you think man-on-man is hot?

180. Have you ever let an animal lick your skin to the point that it began to turn you on?

181. Have you ever come on to your doctor?

182. Have you ever tried to get it on with your therapist?

183. Have you ever washed a lover in the shower spending a great deal of time soaping them up in or about their private places?

184. Have you ever lied to anyone about what you do for a living to get them into the sack?

185. Have you ever had sex in the out-of-doors?

186. Have you ever performed oral sex in a locker room?

187. Have you ever received oral sex in a locker room?

188. Have you ever gone out with someone solely because they seemed to have big boobs or a large penis?

189. Have you ever hung upside down with the blood flowing to your head to achieve a better orgasm?

190. Have you ever licked anyone's butt hole?

191. Have you ever had a fist either up your own or someone else's vagina?

192. How about up your own or someone else's asshole?

193. Have you ever had sex with someone you knew had HPV (genital warts)?

194. Have you ever had sex with someone you knew had herpes?

195. Have you ever had sex with someone because they were rich or famous?

196. Did you ever perform any sex acts beyond kissing during a game (like Truth or Dare)?

197. Have you ever masturbated next to your partner while they were asleep?

198. Have you ever had sex while cross-dressed?

199. Have you ever dressed up in a costume for sex?

200. Have you ever used common household items as sex toys (like a spatula)?

201. Have you ever role-played that you were a victim or perpetrator of a sex crime with a partner?

202. Have you ever gotten a blowjob from or given a blowjob to a person with their/your tongue pierced?

203. Did you ever call a lover "Mama" or "Big Daddy" during intimate relations?

204. Have you ever imagined that you were with a celebrity while you were fucking your partner?

205. Have you ever imagined you were with someone of a sex opposite that of your partner while you were having sex?

206. Have you ever pretended to have sex with the significant other of your sibling?

207. Have you ever had sex with someone who you knew was only having sex with you because of your performance on a stage, in a movie or TV show, or on an athletic field?

208. Have you ever been fucked in the ass by a dildo?

209. Have you ever fucked someone in the ass with a dildo?

210. Have you ever sat down on an erect penis?

211. Have you ever somehow gotten left tied up or in handcuffs during or after sex?

212. Ever licked alcohol off someone's body?

213. Have you ever needed lubricant because yours or your partner's penis was too big to go in without it?

214. Have you ever put a vibrator up your own ass?

215. Have you ever had sex doggy style?

216. Ever had sex on a swing?

217. Have you ever modeled sex after something you read in a book?

218. How about modeled sex after something you saw in a movie?

219. Have you ever woken up to someone having sex with you?

220. Ever woken up anyone by performing oral sex on them?

221. Have you ever received oral sex by two or more people at one time?

222. Ever had sex on hay?

223. Ever had sex in the snow?

224. Ever had sex in mud?

225. How about on concrete?

226. On sand?

227. Ever given or received oral sex on a beach?

228. How about at the pool under a towel?

229. Have you ever achieved orgasm from rubbing yourself with sand?

230. Ever put your dick in a Guinness beer because the foamy head looked so inviting (and if you don't

have a dick, have you ever thought that if you did you'd want to fuck the foamy head of a Guinness)?

231. Ever had "girl on top" sex?

232. Ever had sex with both of you standing up?

233. Ever done 69?

234. Have you ever called out someone's name, other than your sex partner's in the middle of the act?

235. Have you and your partner ever taken anyone home from a bar to have sex with together?

236. Have you or your partner ever been on their period while you had sex?

237. Did you or your partner ever *get* a period *during* sex?

238. Has seeing the erect penis of a large animal, like a horse or a whale, ever gotten you aroused?

239. Has the hot breath of an animal on your neck or other exposed skin ever turned you on?

240. Have you ever masturbated while watching people having sex through a telescope or out a window?

241. Have you ever had sex with a partner who was in the hospital or with someone visiting you in the hospital?

242. Have you ever had something in two holes at once?

243. Ever fallen asleep during sex?

244. Have you ever had sex with a complete stranger?

245. Have you ever received a "happy ending" after a massage?

246. Are there people you have had sex with that you cannot name?

247. Have you ever needed an introduction to someone you had slept with when you ran into them at a later date?

248. Can you turn yourself on by watching yourself dance naked in a mirror?

249. Did you ever have a pillow you kept solely for purposes of masturbation because the fabric had become worn on the corners from rubbing against it?

250. Ever had a sock you kept for masturbation that you never let your mother wash?

251. Were you ever the first one to take your clothes off at a party or in a bar just because you were drunk enough and felt like being naked?

252. The first time you had sex, did you initiate?

253. Have you ever been forced to have sex and enjoyed it on any level?

254. Have you ever been begged for sex?

255. Have you ever begged for sex?

256. Have you ever licked up semen off your own hand?

257. Have you licked it off someone else's body?

258. Have you ever sucked pussy off of someone else's mouth or penis?

259. Have you ever done a strip tease in front of more than one person?

260. Have you ever done a strip tease for a person of the same sex?

261. Have you ever inserted a Barbie or Ken doll into any orifice of your body?

262. Have you ever had sex with a hermaphrodite?

263. How about a transgender person (pre- or post-op)?

264. Have you ever had sex at your office during work hours?

265. Have you ever inserted any fruits or vegetables inside yourself?

266. Has anyone ever inserted fruits or vegetables for you?

267. And while we're at it, have you ever inserted vegetables into someone else?

268. Have you ever fucked someone immediately after they had been fucked by someone else?

269. Do you know, off the top of your head, the color of your most recent sex partner's asshole?

270. Have you ever forced yourself sexually on another person?

271. Have you ever had sex with someone delivering something to you?

272. Have you ever had sex with someone more than twenty years older than you?

273. Have you ever had sex with someone more than twenty years younger than you?

274. Have you ever had sexual relations with the bartender while they were on their shift at a bar?

275. Ever had sex in your parents' bed?

276. Ever borrowed a condom from your sibling?

277. How about from your parents?

278. Ever had sex in the bedroom of your child or the child of your partner (without the child present, hopefully!)?

279. Ever cleaned up after sex using an article of clothing that did not belong to you or your partner (like your roommate's T-shirt)?

280. Ever had sex with an Amish person?

281. Ever had sex with a fundamentalist Christian virgin?

282. How about an Orthodox Jew?

283. Ever fucked a devout Muslim?

284. An apple pie?

285. Or a snake hole?

286. Have you ever stolen a porno?

287. Have you ever watched a porn movie that

involved animals, people dressed as animals, or animal excrement?

288. Have you ever sucked two cocks at once?

289. Have you ever had more than one cock in more than one hole at one time?

290. Have you ever made one of your siblings cum that you know of?

291. Have you ever made out in public and been caught by a stranger?

292. Have you ever had sexual intercourse in public and been caught by a stranger?

293. Have you ever solicited sex in a bathroom?

294. Have you ever applied a food spread (like peanut butter) to a private part of your body to encourage a person to lick you there?

295. How about to encourage an animal to lick you there?

296. Have you ever refused to perform oral sex because your partner smelled bad?

297. Have you ever had sex with a correctional officer while in jail?

298. Have you ever had sex in a small local park with kids' laughter ringing through the air in the background?

299. Have you ever had sex on school property during the day when school was in session?

300. Have you ever injured anyone or been injured during sex?

301. Have you ever made out in a church, temple, or mosque?

302. Have you actually had sex in a church, temple, or mosque?

303. Have you ever bitten someone's nipples until they bled?

304. Have you ever hung weights from your nipples?

305. Have you ever asphyxiated yourself during an orgasm?

306. Have you ever had sex with someone you knew had AIDS?

307. Have you ever had sex with a ghost (as in "poltergeist")?

308. Have you ever masturbated in the same bed as a sleeping family member?

309. Have you ever had sex with a religious or spiritual leader?

310. Have you ever role-played that you were the mother or father of your sex partner?

311. Have you ever had sex with a student of yours (who was of age)?

312. Have you ever had sex with someone as they berated you verbally?

313. Have you ever been hit or otherwise abused during sex?

314. Have you ever had sex with an animal?

315. Have you ever had sex with a corpse?

316. Have you ever fucked someone in their cheek dimple?

317. How about in their ear?

318. Have you ever used a strap-on during sex?

319. Have you ever used a cock ring during sex?

320. Have you ever stuck a cush ball up your ass and "pooped" it out and enjoyed it?

321. Have you ever had water or orange juice poured on you during sex to simulate urination?

322. Have you ever poured a liquid over a partner to simulate urination?

323. Have you ever held a vibrator against yourself while being fucked?

324. Have you ever held a vibrator against your partner's asshole while they came?

325. Have you ever performed oral sex on anyone in your immediate family?

326. Have you ever had sex with a sibling and a third party?

327. Ever made out with your babysitter?

328. Ever gotten laid by your babysitter?

329. Have you ever slept with your kid's babysitter?

330. Have you ever accidentally killed or almost killed someone during sex?

331. Have you ever used food as a lubricant during sex?

332. Have you ever been chained up like a dog and insulted as part of a sex game?

333. Have you ever whipped anyone during sex?

334. Ever incorporated an actual weapon into your sex practices (including a whip)?

335. Ever gotten a "devil's smile" eating a girl out while she was on her period?

336. Have you ever posted yourself on the Internet having sex?

337. Have you ever begged for sex?

338. Have you ever had sex with a Real Doll?

339. Have you ever had sex while dancing?

340. Have you ever "titty-fucked"?

341. Have you ever fucked in a hot tub or a swimming pool?

342. Ever inserted the heel of a stiletto into your asshole?

343. Have you ever staged the murder of either you or your partner to turn one or both of you on?

344. Have you ever frozen your shit for someone else to fuck themselves with?

345. Have you ever eaten someone else's shit?

346. Have you ever been really turned on by a really hairy ass or pubic region or armpit?

347. Have you ever had sex with someone you met over a sex hotline or in a personal ad?

348. Ever squirted or been with a girl who squirted during an orgasm?

349. Ever projectiled cum more than five feet or been with someone who did?

350. Ever been in a circle fuck?

351. Have you ever gone to a swingers' club and traded partners?

352. Have you ever done it at a key party?

353. Have you ever had sex with a steward or stewardess on an airplane?

354. How about the pilot?

355. Did you ever borrow sex toys from your parents?

356. Have you ever eaten anything out of the butt crack of any of your lovers?

357. Have you ever had sex in a group of more than two people where you were of the same sex of at least one other person?

358. Have you ever role-played that you rescued your partner from a dangerous situation before sex?

359. Ever had sex at a brothel?

360. Ever had sex with a prostitute in a foreign country?

361. Have you ever had sex on a roommate's bed with someone other than your roommate?

362. Ever had sex with your roommate?

363. Ever had sex with a good friend's immediate family member?

364. Have you ever had sex with a coworker?

365. How about your boss?

366. Ever have sex with someone you could fire if you wanted to?

367. Ever fired someone for not sleeping with you?

368. Have you ever had sex with any of your medical doctors?

369. Ever been a little turned on by your gynecologist during an exam?

370. For the boys: ever been a little turned on by the idea of your girlfriend getting a gyno exam?

371. Ever had sex in a theater? (Backstage counts!)

372. Have you ever had sex outside in the rain?

373. Have you ever had sex with two members of the same family?

374. Have you ever sung or been sung to while having sex?

375. Have you ever been genuinely laughing while reaching orgasm?

376. Have you ever had sex with someone really funny who made you laugh so much you had to stop the sex to pull it together?

377. Have you ever had sex while both of you had your hands tied behind your back?

378. Have you ever given or received a hummer?

379. Have you or your partner ever lost an erection during sex?

380. Have you ever been able to get that person hard again minutes after they lost it?

381. Have you ever had sex at a bowling alley?

382. On a football field?

383. On a tennis court?

384. Or a baseball diamond?

385. Ever had sex on top of a board game you had been in the middle of playing?

386. Ever arrived at someone's house, fucked them, and left all in the space of an hour?

387. Ever arrived naked under a coat to someone's house with whom you hoped to have sex?

388. Ever had anyone show up to your house naked under a coat?

389. Have you ever arrived home to your partner naked, waiting to have sex?

390. Ever had to "ice" your genitals after a particularly boisterous sex session?

391. Have you ever had sex at a museum?

392. Ever painted someone's skin for purposes of foreplay?

393. Ever forced a partner into a "dutch oven" and pissed them off to the point that they refused you sex (or offered it to make you stop)?

394. Ever had sex with a politician?

395. Have you ever joined a club or taken a class to get closer to someone you were hoping to have sex with?

396. Have you ever had sex in rhythm to the music you had playing in the background?

397. Have you ever fucked a grapefruit? (Be honest . . .)

398. Has the dungeon master in your game of D&D ever offered points for sex?

399. Ever had Avatar sex?

400. Did this test make you want to go have sex? (Are you thinking, what doesn't make me want to have sex? In which case, give yourself a "yes.")

YOUR SEXUAL PURITY NUMBER:
_____%

The Drug
Purity Test

Psychedelics, downers, and stimulants, oh my! It's impossible to determine with certainty when human beings first used drugs, and whether or not that initial use was medicinal, recreational, spiritual, or all three. The only thing we know for sure is that it was a really, really long time ago. The first practitioners of perception-modification probably celebrated a profitable night's work by rolling a fattie.

People have consumed alcohol since before our earliest records. Coffee arrived a bit later; we can trace the first hot cups of joe to Ethiopia in the ninth century. Ever since humans abandoned their nomadic roots for the relatively dull agricultural life, they've been looking for ways to get fucked up out of sheer boredom.

Alcohol has always played a central role in religious

practices. From Communion, where wine represents the blood of Christ, to the kiddush, where a glass of wine is blessed during the welcoming of the Sabbath, alcohol in the Judeo-Christian tradition symbolizes a connection to a higher power, or perhaps to our spiritual selves. In Islam, on the other hand, alcohol is banned due to the sinful barrier it puts between people and their best selves.

In fact, throughout history alcohol has been loathed as much as it has been loved. Well-meaning anti-alcohol activists managed to convince the government to enact Prohibition in 1920, outlawing alcohol—and leading organized crime to flourish until it ended. Even today, one county might be "dry" while its neighboring county features twice the usual number of bars and liquor stores to accommodate the extra business.

Similarly polarizing are drugs used in recreation and religion alike. Peyote has been used in some Native American rituals throughout the ages. The Rastafarian movement uses ganja (marijuana) as a tool for enlightenment. And worshippers at the altar of Hollywood celebrity use a mystic combination of cocaine and champagne as part of their own dark rituals.

Drugs and alcohol are a mainstay of such highly prized activities as rockin' and rollin', "hanging with the homies," and going on drive-by shootings. They're fun! Sure, drugs are mostly illegal and often render you completely moronic, but they are also *bad*! And, bad is the new good! Here in America, drugs are impure, even if they are cooler than all hell. Even if they do grab you by the short-and-curlies and ruin your life in spectacular fashion, you get to go to a magical place called rehab where they fix you *and* you get to meet young, hot starlets who don't wear underpants!

On to the instructional portion of today's lecture. What are the most popular illegal drugs, and what do they do?

Cannabis (marijuana, ganja, or pot) Can be grown anywhere by anyone if they have fluorescent lights and heat lamps. If you smoke it, it makes you a little slow, but also very funny. Or it just makes you super-paranoid. Or it makes you want to eat things like olives on toast or chocolate-covered ramen noodles. Sometimes it makes you all of these things and more. But the sex, if you remember to have it before you fall asleep, is fantastic!

Cocaine A stimulant that makes you feel really great and powerful for about ten minutes, then hate and loathe yourself. However, if you do more, you will continue to feel great. But if you ever want to sleep again, you have to stop eventually, and then your self-loathing and hatred will be directly proportional to how long it took you to stop doing coke. If you do this drug, hide all sharp objects beneath self-help books about finding the will to live.

Dimethyltryptamine (DMT) A psychedelic drug used by indigenous cultures for ages. People who've taken it say it opens a portal to a parallel universe. So dress warmly.

Richard the Purity Gerbil says:

This is the drug section, and if it doesn't make you pass out or dance on top of a bar in front of your boss at the annual office party, you are probably doing something very wrong. First, find yourself a fat, healthy vein and get ready to mainline some knowledge.

Rule 1: In the spirit of all the tests in this book, be aware that if you come across a question like "Have you ever combined GHB with alcohol and thrown up?" and you think, "I've taken G with alcohol, but I didn't get sick. I just kind of felt like something was crawling on me," or something similar, you can give yourself a *yes* based on the "Or Something Similar" clause.

Gamma-Hydroxybutyric acid (GHB) A cheap synthetic depressant that puts you in a coma, gives you temporary amnesia, or kills you. Or, maybe, it'll make you giddy and "drunk times a thousand," as they say. So good luck with that grab bag.

Lysergic acid diethylamide (LSD) A synthetic hallucinogen that will make you see gnomes in your soup for

Rule #2: Scores for this section are as easy to obtain as marijuana at a rock show:

* Keep track of your *no* answers.
* Divide your total after 400 questions by 4.
* Drop any decimals or remainders.
* Add a percentage.
* *Example: 290 no answers divided by 4 is 72.5, which makes your Purity Number 72 percent.*

If you feel confused about anything, wait six hours and drink a lot of water. That should help. Maybe eat something.

Okay. Now who's got a lighter?

at least twelve hours. When LSD is fun, it's fun. When it sucks, you're locked in your head like Rapunzel, except the prince is an upside-down neon clown, and all your hair fell out and turned into spaghetti.

Methamphetamine (crystal meth) Usually cooked up by the genius who blew up that old abandoned house around the corner. Crystal meth is a stimulant that addicts tend to choose over personal hygiene—their teeth fall out—or their own children. To be fair, it keeps you dancing better than Red Bull. Dancing on your own grave, that is.

Oxycodone (Percocet, Percodan) A depressant and pain-killer that, when used recreationally, can either make you feel really good or make it hard to breathe. If you're going to drink alcohol with this too, you might as well put on a nice outfit. Nothing worse than being found dead in a hotel room wearing last year's jeans.

Ketamine (Special K) Known to have disassociative properties (also known as "I am seeing swirlies in my Cheerios"), Special K is used to tranquilize both horses and club-goers. It can cause seizures, amnesia, and death, but don't let that affect your decision if you're a vet looking for a good horse tranquilizer.

1. Have you ever puffed on candy cigarettes and enjoyed it?

2. Have you ever sat in a room enjoying other people's secondhand smoke?

3. Were you under the age of ten the first time you tasted any alcoholic beverage?

4. Have you ever owned smoking paraphernalia? Papers? A pipe? A bong?

5. Did you know what a bong was before college?

6. Did you ever smoke a cigarette before college?

7. Have you hung out for a night with people getting drunk while you stayed sober?

8. Have you ever woken up horrified by something you'd done the night before?

9. Have you ever thrown up from too much alcohol?

10. Did you ever forget something you did or said after a big night out for several days and only remember when another person (or photo) reminded you?

11. Did you ever drink a caffeinated beverage to help you stay up later than normal?

12. Do you like nighttime better than morning?

13. When you see someone mumbling to themselves and acting disoriented on the street, do you immediately assume they are on some kind of drug rather than mentally imbalanced or just stressed out?

14. Have you ever taken a drug to help you lose weight?

15. Do you take at least one vitamin per week?

16. Do you think vitamins are an example of an industry that hired a great PR firm but whose credibility is otherwise completely suspect?

17. How about herbs in general? Is it all a bunch of bullshit?

18. Have you ever taken more than the recommended dose of any over-the-counter medication?

19. Have you ever seen your parents (one or both) drunk?

20. Have you ever smoked a clove cigarette?

21. Have you ever held your breath until you were light-headed?

22. Have you ever sniffed a marker or a pen until you were light-headed?

23. Have you ever enjoyed pumping gas because of the smell?

24. Have you ever stayed up all night partying?

25. Have you ever rolled a joint?

26. Have you ever mixed a drink with more than three types of alcohol and drank it?

27. Do you know the recipe for at least one cocktail off the top of your head?

28. Have you ever lied to a doctor about smoking cigarettes? (Like telling him/her you NEVER smoke when "never" really means only on the weekends?)

29. Have you ever smoked a cigarette that was "natural" or "nicotine free?"

30. Does the idea of rolling a cigarette seem "better for you" than one out of a box?

31. Have you ever used a can of whipped cream to do a whippit?

32. Have you ever taken prescription medication prescribed to you after you were all better?

33. Were you ever prescribed a medication for one ailment and taken it for another? (For example: a painkiller meant for oral pain taken for a headache?)

34. Have you ever had an extra drink or two so that you could "loosen yourself up"?

35. Have you ever smoked a joint because you knew it would make the movie you were watching a whole lot better?

36. Have you ever felt jealous watching other people who were high or drunk and wished you could join them? (For example, while you were working at a bar and sober as a church mouse?)

37. Have you ever had a beer or a hit off a joint to impress someone you liked?

38. Have you ever had a drink to help you fall asleep more easily?

39. Have you ever taken a spoonful of NyQuil to help you sleep when you *didn't* have a cold?

40. Do you take a painkiller (Advil, aspirin, etc.) pretty much every time you have a headache?

41. Are you totally comfortable taking antacids for stomach/digestive issues?

42. Do you take painkillers if you ever wake up with a hangover?

43. Do you think sleep and water are the best hangover cures?

44. Have you ever taken a shot of alcohol off of someone's body?

45. Have you ever had to act more sober than you were because the people around you wouldn't approve?

46. Have you ever lied about how much you drank or smoked?

47. Have you ever had a cup of Coca-Cola and claimed there was rum in it to avoid peer pressure?

48. Have you ever pretended to hit a joint or a cigarette to feel cool without actually inhaling?

49. Have you ever tried to get a friend higher or drunker to have someone keeping up with you?

50. Have you ever bought a round of drinks for people as an excuse to keep drinking?

51. Have you ever taken a shot of something without knowing what it was?

52. Have you ever gotten a tattoo while high or drunk?

53. Have you ever smoked hash?

54. Have you ever smuggled more than the legal amount of tax-free cigarettes into the country? (Two hundred smokes is the legal limit in the United States.)

55. Have you ever flown domestically with marijuana on your person?

56. Have you ever taken a cigarette hit out of someone else's mouth?

57. Have you ever urinated outside while drunk?

58. Have you ever told anyone you loved them while heavily intoxicated?

59. Have you ever watched *The Wizard of Oz* muted while listening to Pink Floyd's *Dark Side of the Moon* while stoned and decided it was TOTALLY WRITTEN FOR IT?

60. Have you ever been high and decided that the people on the news were all high too?

61. Have you ever "babysat" for friends while they were tripping on acid?

62. Ever taken E?

63. Have you ever baked pot cookies or brownies?

64. Have you ever eaten pot cookies or brownies?

65. Have you ever had the munchies and found yourself eating things you'd never eat sober (i.e. dry pasta and ketchup)?

66. Have you ever grown pot?

67. Have you ever brewed your own beer?

68. Have you ever distilled your own wine?

69. Have you ever been vomited on by a wasted person?

70. Have you ever puked after getting drunk and then smoking a joint?

71. Do you ever use inhalers or nasal spray when you aren't sick?

72. Have you ever drunk absinthe?

73. Have you ever taken drugs and played a musical instrument or sang?

74. Have you ever been high or drunk while on a boat?

75. Have you ever sniffed nail polish to get high?

76. Have you ever had a glass or two of wine to help you write something creative?

77. Have you ever tripped in order to expand your creative mind?

78. Have you ever gone on a bar crawl? (A "bar

crawl" is when you go bar to bar and have a drink or two at each . . . as if you didn't know.)

79. Have you ever been high and written something (a song, a play, a story) that you believed to be the greatest thing ever, only to sober up and realize it sucked?

80. Have you ever shotgunned a beer out of a beer bong?

81. Have you ever enjoyed a healthy game of beer pong?

82. Have you ever pulled an "Irish exit" (where you are so drunk at the end of the night you just slip out without saying good-bye)?

83. Have you ever had a Jell-O shot?

84. Ever done an orgasm shot in public?

85. Ever done an Irish Car Bomb?

86. Have you ever done Triple C (cold medicine) recreationally?

87. Have you ever been so burnt out that you had trouble stringing together a sentence?

88. Have you ever smoked around a pregnant person?

89. Do you know how to measure out bags of marijuana?

90. Do you know how to measure out cocaine?

91. Have you ever cleaned your whole house while drunk or high?

92. Have you ever bought more than an eighth of pot at a time?

93. Did you ever watch a cartoon stoned and announce out loud that the makers of the program *had* to be high?

94. Did you ever drive a car stoned?

95. Have you ever run outside during a full moon, stripped off your clothes, and howled while wasted?

96. Have you ever danced on a table drunk?

97. Have you ever gone on and on about (something like) how astrology is totally the world's oldest science and that the moon affects water and humans are made up of mostly water and therefore you have never met anyone with more Leo characteristics than you, while drunk or high?

98. Have you ever cleared a room with your singing voice during a drunken night of karaoke?

99. To your drunken dismay, have you ever made a whole group of stoned people play a game together because you felt like they'd really get into it once they got going?

100. Have you ever realized you and a friend had nothing in common anymore once they became a stoner and you became a drunk?

101. Have you ever woken up and needed to drink more than three glasses of water within the first minute of consciousness?

102. Did you ever steal cigarettes? (Taking them out of your mom's purse is stealing.)

103. Have you ever smoked at least one pack of cigarettes (twenty) in one night?

104. Did you ever steal alcohol? (And yes, the alcohol cabinet in a friend's parent's basement is probably stealing unless you think your friend's dad wouldn't mind sharing with his fifteen-year-old son or daughter's friend.)

105. Do you know how to prepare more than three kinds of cocktails?

106. Have you been drunk while the sun was still out?

107. Have you ever been high in the daytime?

108. Did you ever smoke more than a pack of cigarettes in a single day?

109. Have you ever been the only one getting wasted in a group of sober people?

110. Have you ever combined more than one mind-altering substance at one time? (Like caffeine and alcohol or pot and acid?)

111. Have you ever blacked out from mind-altering substances?

112. Have you ever stayed up all night with the assistance of drugs to keep you awake? (And yes, coffee counts . . .)

113. Did you ever take a drug to help you study for a test?

114. Have you ever gotten a headache from sniffing glue or pens long before you got a buzz?

115. When you've watched *Alice in Wonderland,* did you figure out on your own that the mushrooms she eats are probably hallucinogenic before someone else mentioned it?

116. Have you ever taken an over-the-counter medication to the point where you are hallucinating or are decidedly high?

117. Have you ever taken Ritalin recreationally?

118. Did you ever get into an argument because drugs or alcohol made you feel belligerent?

119. Have you ever gotten wasted with a sibling?

120. Have you ever passed on a joint because someone else smoking it grossed you out?

121. Have you ever gotten stiffed on a bag of pot, arriving home to discover a bag of pine needles or oregano?

122. Have you ever smoked something without knowing what it was?

123. Have you ever smoked cigarettes in a car with minor children riding in it?

124. Have you ever huffed glue?

125. Have you ever left a mark on your face (likely, below your nose) from sniffing something for a high and not known about it for any period of time?

126. Have you ever done a whippit from a balloon made from a nitrous oxide tank?

127. Have you ever flattened more than five cans of whipped cream in one night doing whippits?

128. Have you ever been fired from a job at an ice cream parlor for sucking all the nitrous out of cans of whipped cream?

129. Have you ever been fired from a job at a pharmacy or a doctor's office (etc.) for stealing medication and/or drugs of any kind?

130. Have you ever taken someone else's prescription drugs for recreational purposes?

131. Have you ever put alcohol in a pet's water dish to try to get it drunk?

132. Have you ever blown pot smoke at a pet to try to get it high?

133. Have you ever tried to get someone high or drunk so that you would have a better chance of getting in their pants?

134. Have you ever gotten drunk to get rid of a hangover?

135. Have you ever smoked pot out of a fruit or vegetable?

136. Can you describe at least one way to get into a corked bottle of wine without using a corkscrew or wine key?

137. Have ever snorted cocaine so that you could be more fun at a party?

138. Have you ever snorted cocaine to make you feel less drunk?

139. Did you ever take ecstasy for the sole purpose of having better sex?

140. Have you ever gotten high on any drug to see what it would be like to have sex on it?

141. Have you ever taken a hit of pot out of someone else's mouth (i.e., "shotgunned" it)?

142. Have you ever been given drugs as payment for a performance (i.e., a rock show, a play, a poem)?

143. Have you ever written a song or a poem in homage to a drug or drink?

144. Have you ever thought that you love a drug or a drink more than anything else in the world? (The answer is "yes" even if in the sober light of day the feeling passed . . .)

145. Did you ever want a drug more than the company of a friend or loved one?

146. Did you ever have a fight with a friend or loved one because they were doing too many drugs or drinking too much?

147. Did you ever have a fight with a friend or loved one because *you* were doing too many drugs or drinking too much?

148. Have you ever gotten drunk or high in order to improve a performance, either on stage or at a party?

149. Have you ever been tripping on acid in front of your boyfriend or girlfriend's family?

150. Have you ever drunk dialed someone you liked and completely humiliated yourself?

151. Have you ever smoked a joint on a playground or on school grounds?

152. Have you ever taken crystal meth?

153. Have you ever made your own crystal meth?

154. Have you ever referred to yourself as a "tweeker?"

155. Ever referred to someone you consider a friend as a "tweeker?"

156. To the best of your knowledge, has anyone ever referred to you as a "tweeker" when they weren't kidding?

157. Have you ever licked the mirror trying to pick up traces of cocaine or has it ever occurred to you to do so?

158. Have you ever popped a pill without knowing what it was?

159. Ever taken G?

160. Do you think Rastafarianism is onto something in using marijuana as a tool for achieving spiritual enlightenment?

161. Have you ever been wasted and woken up having adopted a pet (like a dog or a cat)?

162. Have you ever woken up after a night of partying with a new job?

163. How about with a new girlfriend/boyfriend?

164. Have you ever crossed an international border with drugs stashed in a bottle of shampoo?

165. Have you ever accidentally flown internationally with drugs on your person?

166. Have you ever smoked pot with your mother or father?

167. Have you ever forgotten the name of your partner while high?

168. Did you ever urinate in a closet while drunk thinking it was the bathroom?

169. Have you ever peed in your pants while wasted?

170. Have you ever drooled while wasted and wide awake?

171. Have you ever used a marijuana vaporizer?

172. Have you ever gotten drunk by yourself?

173. How about high?

174. Ever done cocaine without telling anyone you were doing it?

175. Acid?

176. Have you ever taken magic mushrooms?

177. Have you ever taken mushrooms by yourself?

178. Have you ever taken so much acid in a given week you forgot which reality you inhabited at a given moment?

179. Have you ever tripped at a Grateful Dead show (or a Phish show if you were born in the 1980s)?

180. Have you ever bought drugs at a concert and taken them?

181. Ever faked sobriety while at work?

182. How about with your grandparents?

183. Have you ever snuck out of your parents' house to do drugs?

184. Have you ever stood outside in a rainstorm to smoke a cigarette?

185. Ever stood outside in a T-shirt during a blizzard to smoke?

186. Ever snuck a cigarette in an airplane or airport bathroom?

187. Have you ever secretly smoked a cigarette in a bar where it was illegal to smoke?

188. Ever been kicked out of a bar for smoking?

189. Have you ever smoked a cigarette in the stairwell of your apartment building because you didn't feel like going outside?

190. Ever snuck a cigarette out of the window of a person's home who would have been really pissed off about you smoking in their home?

191. Have you ever been wasted at a funeral?

192. How about at a wedding?

193. Ever been called in to work while you were drunk or high?

194. Ever called off work because you were drunk or high?

195. Have you ever taken Ritalin to help you study or finish an important project?

196. Have you ever taken crack?

197. Have you ever scraped a marijuana pipe to smoke the resin?

198. Have you ever blipped (inhaled a small amount of cocaine)?

199. Ever had Everclear?

200. Ever made your own Everclear?

201. Have you ever smoked pot as a medicinal pain reliever?

202. Do you have any pot or cocaine dealers' numbers saved in your phone?

203. Have you ever mixed a cocktail in a thermos or bottle covered with cartoon characters?

204. Have you ever drunk alcohol out of a flask?

205. Ever had a beer in a paper bag?

206. Have you ever gotten high with a teacher or professor?

207. Have you ever broken up with someone because they were using too many drugs?

208. Have you ever forgotten to feed a pet because you were too high to remember?

209. Have you ever smoked cigarettes, pot, or anything else indoors around minors?

210. Have you ever confiscated someone else's booze or drugs (like students at the school where you teach or campers at the camp where you work) and then taken them yourself?

211. Have you ever blatantly refused to join an anti-drug organization or otherwise refused to campaign against drugs even though you were invited to do so?

212. Have you ever idolized Jim Morrison?

213. Have you ever smoked opium?

214. Have you ever bought a drug that you had no idea how to take?

215. Have you ever thought that the book *Go Ask Alice* totally understands adolescent drug use?

216. Have you ever organized a party around a drug-related theme?

217. Did you always "get" what was happening to Dorothy in *The Wizard of Oz* scene where they fall asleep under the poppy dust?

218. Have you ever had a beer you paid more than six dollars for?

219. Ever spent ten dollars or more on a cocktail?

220. Can you name the restaurant with the best brunch-time Bloody Mary in your neighborhood?

221. Have you ever made the sober claim that you are an amazing driver when you are high?

222. Have you ever driven while tripping and forgot momentarily that you were the driver?

223. Have you ever started eating food while tripping on acid and thought for a moment that you had forgotten how to swallow?

224. Have you ever gone swimming while tripping on acid and forgotten momentarily that you could not in fact *breathe* under water?

225. Have you ever fallen in the toilet while drunk or high?

226. Have you ever had an echo come back to you while you were fucked up and you thought it was someone calling from the other side of a canyon?

227. Have you ever failed a drug test?

228. Have you ever been drug tested while completely fucked up?

229. Have you ever thought, "I *am* the Jabberwocky!"?

230. Have you ever stolen money or items of value for drugs?

231. Have you ever had to hide from cops? (Paranoid delusional hiding counts too!)

232. Have you ever been high during waking hours in excess of twenty-four hours?

233. Have you ever had to go to the hospital while high?

234. Can you name at least three images that commonly appear on pages of acid tabs?*

235. Did you ever try shooting up or snorting something from your kitchen or bathroom just to see if it would get you high?

236. How about drinking or eating it?

---

* Jesus, American flag, and swirlies. (We will also accept flowers, nature scenes, and "What are you talking about?")

237. Ever smoked a random household item to see its effect?

238. Have you ever hung out for a night with people shooting up heroin while you stayed sober just because you were curious to see what it looked like?

239. Have you ever mixed more than three types of mind-altering substances at one time?

240. Have you ever had the thought, "I am going to die right now," while high or drunk?

241. Have you ever stayed awake for more than forty-eight hours with the assistance of drugs or alcohol?

242. Did you ever have sex using a sexual enhancement drug (like Viagra) before the age of forty?

243. Have you ever smoked two packs of cigarettes (forty) or more in a night?

244. Have you ever used drugs to help you win any athletic events?

245. Have you ever gotten into a fistfight because a drug made you feel belligerent?

246. Have you ever exchanged sex for drugs or vice versa?

247. Have you ever pinched out of your friends' bags of drugs after you scored it for them?

248. Have you ever lost your stash of drugs only to rediscover it again months later?

249. How about a year or more later?

250. Have you ever lost your stash in the lining of a coat or bag only to have it rediscovered by a child or parent?

251. Have you ever gotten wasted in front of your parents?

252. How about your grandparents?

253. Ever gotten hammered *with* your parents?

254. Grandparents?

255. Have you ever stiffed anyone on a bag of drugs by replacing them with herbs, baby powder, or some other household item?

256. Have you ever drunk the bong water? (By accident or to win a dare both count!)

257. Have you ever snorted anything before you knew what it was?

258. Have you ever injected anything before you knew what it was?

259. Did you ever look at your coffee table on the morning after a big party and think to yourself, "Lord help me" or something similar?

260. Have you ever lied to a doctor about the amount of drugs you do? (For example, if you say you don't do drugs and you just got off a coke binge, that would be lying.)

261. Have you ever opened your gas tank and huffed? (Inhaling deeply counts . . .)

262. Have you ever passed out from a whippit?

263. Have you ever passed out from huffing gasoline?

264. Have you ever been sent home from work for being high or drunk while on the job?

265. Ever been "sat down" by an employer who was "concerned" about you?

266. Have you ever been fired from a job for being high or drunk too often?

267. Did you ever quit a job so that you could go to a party or just go home and get wasted?

268. Were you ever wasted while operating heavy machinery?

269. Have you ever been high or drunk while babysitting or watching someone else's children?

270. Have you ever been high or drunk while watching your own children?

271. Have you ever given a pet acid or mushrooms?

272. Have you ever injected a pet with heroin?

273. Have you ever given someone under the age of thirteen drugs or alcohol?

274. Have you ever slipped anyone a roofie?

275. Have you ever given someone acid without their knowledge?

276. Have you ever snuck someone, without their knowledge, extra drugs or alcohol to get them in the sack?

277. Have you ever snorted cocaine to make a better impression at a job interview?

278. Have you ever taken a roofie on purpose or asked your partner to take one?

279. Have you ever gotten high on any drug to see what it would be like to drive while on it?

280. Have you ever done a line of cocaine off of someone's body?

281. Have you ever been forced to do a drug that you didn't want to do?

282. Did you ever force someone to do a drug that they didn't want to do?

283. Have you ever begged someone for drugs?

284. Have you ever bought drugs on "credit" because you were too broke to pay at the time you wanted them?

285. Has anyone ever come after you for drug money that you owed them?

286. Have you ever been too wasted to go out and get your own drugs or alcohol and enlisted someone else to go get them for you?

287. Have you ever been given drugs in exchange for a favor or for doing a job for someone else?

288. Have you ever taken more than two tabs of acid at a time?

289. Have you ever woken up and had no idea where you were?

290. Have you ever been in a drug-related shoot-out?

291. Did you ever smoke cigarettes in your high school bathroom?

292. Ever smoke them anywhere inside your high school?

293. How about inside your church, synagogue, mosque, or other religious institution?

294. Did you ever get drunk on school property in high school?

295. Did you ever smoke pot outside your high school?

296. Ever show up at your high school wasted after drinking in yours or a friend's car?

297. How about after smoking pot?

298. Did you ever shoot up in the bathroom of your high school?

299. Did you ever trip on acid during the school day when you were in high school?

300. Have you ever had your voice change due to steroid use?

301. Have you ever designed a drug of your own from household supplies that made you or someone you know hallucinate?

302. Have you ever experienced a psychotic break or severe "episode" while fucked up?

303. Did it ever last after the drug was out of your system for any period of time?

304. Have you ever harmed anyone in a fire caused by your meth lab?

305. Have you ever snorted something without ever finding out what you were snorting?

306. Have you ever taken Special K (horse tranquilizer)?

307. Have you ever used peyote in a religious practice?

308. Have you ever been on a DMT trip that took you into an actual parallel universe or to the mother ship?

309. Have you ever sustained an injury believing you could fly while on a drug trip?

310. Have you ever tried to kill yourself while having a particularly bad trip?

311. Have you ever gotten married while high or drunk?

312. Have you ever gotten pregnant while high or drunk? (Getting someone else pregnant while high or drunk works, too.)

313. Have you ever hidden drugs inside a body cavity?

314. Have you ever taken (as in smoked, injected, snorted, drunk, or eaten) all the drugs you had on you

in order to hide them from someone (like the cops or your parents)?

315. Have you ever taken a hit of marijuana out of somebody's vagina?

316. And by that token, how about a hit out of somebody's asshole?

317. Have you ever forgotten your own name while high?

318. Have you ever wet your bed while wasted?

319. Have you ever crapped your pants while particularly fucked up?

320. Have you ever thrown up in anyone's mouth while wasted?

321. Have you ever been sniffed out by a sniffer/detection dog (like at an airport)?

322. Have you ever driven with drugs across state lines?

323. Ever driven with them across the country?

324. Ever received a ticket for marijuana possession?

325. Ever had to go to jail for having a lot of a drug on your person?

326. Have you ever crossed over an American border on foot to get drugs into the U.S.?

327. Ever driven them in?

328. Have you ever robbed an animal hospital to steal the drugs?

329. Ever robbed a pharmacy for drugs?

330. Ever shoplifted over-the-counter drugs to get high?

331. Have you ever gotten a methadone prescription to have on hand just in case you couldn't get heroin?

332. Have you ever gone out after midnight and cruised the streets for drugs out of desperation?

333. Have you ever gotten high on coke vaginally ("balling")?

334. Have you ever been arrested for a drug violation in a foreign country?

335. Have you ever gotten high or drunk with a member of the clergy?

336. Ever gotten high or drunk in a religious institution?

337. Have you ever gone through rehab, left the facility, and immediately scored?

338. Has anyone ever broken up with you and you forgot because you were so high or drunk?

339. Have you ever suffered from cysts or bad acne due to steroid use?

340. Have you ever found yourself unable to stop crying because of the drugs you were on?

341. Have you ever taken ephedrine to stay awake?

342. Have you ever forgotten to feed your baby because you were too drunk or stoned?

343. Have you ever forgotten to pick up your child because you were too fucked up to remember?

344. Have you ever had a drink or smoked a cigarette while pregnant?

345. Have you ever studied for a test drunk and gotten an A?

346. How about an F?

347. Ever bought anyone pregnant a drink or given them a cigarette?

348. Have you ever taken anything you found in someone else's medicine cabinet without asking?

349. Have you ever used alcohol as a painkiller (like to get a tattoo or a piercing)?

350. Have you ever driven drunk or high with minors in the car?

351. Have you ever fallen down and gotten a concussion while high or drunk?

352. Have you ever joined an anti-drug organization and campaigned against drugs while all the while, taking drugs?

353. Have you ever worked at a drug and alcohol rehab and known yourself to have a drug or alcohol problem?

354. Have you ever gone through a drug treatment program just to get out of paying fines?

355. Have you ever dated a drug dealer and done drugs for free as a result?

356. Did you ever deal drugs and therefore get to do them for free?

357. Have you ever dealt drugs and not done them at all?

358. Have you ever gotten a DUI?

359. Have you ever given or received oral sex in exchange for drugs?

360. Have you ever asked for a loan from someone you cared about and lied to them by not disclosing that the money was for drugs?

361. Have you ever gotten drunk while hot-tubbing and passed out from dehydration?

362. Have you ever stopped drinking after getting drunk and endured a terrible headache?

363. Have you ever tried to relieve a headache by drinking alcohol?

364. Ever consumed a whole bottle of wine or more by yourself over dinner?

365. Ever gotten an Indian name while tripping?

366. Did you give it to yourself?

367. Has your family ever "sat you down" to tell you they were "concerned"?

368. Ever had an alcoholic drink out of a fruit rind?

369. Have you ever "overdone it" on the fruity drinks because they barely tasted like alcohol?

370. Do you drink alcohol, or have you ever, through a straw?

371. Have you ever felt what might be called "brand loyalty" to a type of beer?

372. Are you opposed to drinking "well" liquor on principal?

373. Do you have a brand of cigarettes you are committed to buying whenever you've bought cigarettes?

374. Have you ever been a smoker long enough to have been loyal to more than one brand of cigarettes over any period of time?

375. Do you believe you could taste the difference in a blind taste test between a cocktail mixed with a generic vodka over a name-brand vodka?

376. Can you name more than one type of kind bud?

377. Have you ever gone to Humboldt County specifically to try out the chronic?

378. Ever journeyed to Amsterdam to smoke the pot?

379. Ever gone wine tasting in Napa Valley?

380. Have you ever gone to a city for the first time, and without asking, worked out where to buy heroin?

381. Have you ever planned an entire vacation around getting wasted?

382. Ever gone skiing while high or drunk?

383. Have you ever been too high and paranoid to get off the ski lift and ended up riding it back down, or caused a backup because they had to stop it for you?

384. Ever gotten wasted before or while on an amusement park ride?

385. Have you ever gotten on a ride wasted and then freaked out so that they had to stop it and let you off?

386. Have you ever taken Percocet?

387. Have you ever mixed prescription painkillers and alcohol?

388. Ever done so and had an equivalent experience to dance-partying to a Bee Gee's song and really really enjoying it more than you could have ever imagined?

389. Ever told someone you loved them while drunk only to regret it the next day?

390. Have you ever broken up with someone while you were wasted only to regret it the next day?

391. Have you ever told someone you loved them while on Ecstasy only to regret it the next day?

392. Have you ever been so high and paranoid that you walked away from a conversation with another person without an explanation or word of good-bye?

393. Ever rolled on E and decided that all that the world needed was love and water?

394. Have you ever wished you had a million dollars so you could do as much blow as you wanted (after swearing you'd give at least ten grand to children's hunger organizations)?

395. Have you ever stared at yourself in a mirror while fucked up and told yourself you hated yourself?

396. How about the opposite? Ever stared at yourself, completely awed by the fabulous creature that you are?

397. Have you ever gone to the movies high?

398. Ever gone to the movies drunk and been shushed?

399. Has anyone ever called you "Pookie?"

400. After taking this test, do you think someone should?

YOUR DRUG PURITY NUMBER:
_____%

The Criminal Behavior Purity Test

Forget what you've heard. The fact is, it's usually the people *with* jobs who steal the most. In fact, employee theft accounts for half the annual inventory loss in major national retail chains. And who's doing most of the five-finger discounting? Your mom. Forget "those crazy teenagers." Only about 25 percent of shoplifting is done by kids between the ages of thirteen and seventeen. The rest are grown-ups. And studies show that the number of women who steal is on the rise, leaving men in the dust.

But why does crime appeal to these ladies? It's a rush, as anyone who's shoplifted will be happy to tell you. But the truly impure among us avoid the crime drama—after all, the thrill of stolen supermarket beef doesn't really justify getting fucked in the ass and

---

Serial Killer Calling Cards

- Son of Sam left notes for police at the scene of his crimes
- The Washington Sniper left tarot cards
- Charles Manson left messages in blood on the walls of his victims' homes
- Ed Gains left his victims skinned (and then used their skins for lampshades—nice recycling, Ed!)

---

called Marcy at your friendly neighborhood correctional facility. It's about stealth, efficiency, or just using a credit card instead of an inside pocket.

On reaching adulthood, we can no longer focus all of our energy on rebelling against our parents. And everyone likes a little rebellion. So we drive 80 in a 55 mph zone. We chug a Gatorade while cruising the supermarket aisles and toss the bottle before hitting checkout. We do whatever we can to get our hearts pumping. Or we do it because it makes us feel cool, less like the lapdogs to the Man that we truly are.

Tax fraud is rampant among white-collar workers. Taking what you can is the norm for those in the blue-collar world. Just get away with it. That's American

Richard the Purity Gerbil says:

This is just the criminal behavior section, and it requires focus and training. We are not running an amateur ring here, people. We want mad skills, preferably military-based and not straight outta clown school, like some of you bozos. We want you in and out and as slippery as a cat (a cat with an allergy to gerbils). So put down that gun and pick up the pencil.

Like I keep telling you, if you come across a question like "Have you ever been arrested for road rage?" and you think, "I probably should have been," or something similar, you can give yourself a *yes* based on the "Or Something Similar" clause.

In this section, scores are as easy to obtain as a cavity check in maximum security.

- Keep track of your *no* answers.
- Divide your total after 400 questions by 4.
- Drop any decimals or remainders.
- Add a percentage.
- *Example: 290* no *answers divided by 4 is 72.5, which makes your Purity Number 72 percent.*

Remember, if you keep a cool head, we all get out of this alive.

morality at its core: do as you would, but don't get caught because it's unbelievably embarrassing if you do.

1. Have you ever heard a car backfiring and mistaken it for gunshots?

2. Have you ever heard actual gunshots? (Cars backfiring don't count.)

3. Have you ever whistled at anyone walking down the street?

4. Have you ever lived in a neighborhood with a Caucasian minority?

5. Have you ever taken salsa or break-dance lessons?

6. Have you ever met a hooker?

7. Do you know what a five-finger discount is?

8. Have you ever taken something that wasn't yours and used it and put it back without telling anyone about it?

9. Did you ever lie to a parent or authority figure about stealing food when you were little?

10. Have you ever cheated on a test?

11. Have you ever used a fake ID to buy alcohol at a liquor store?

12. Have you ever been in a government building after it was closed?

13. Ever stayed inside a business after closing that you neither worked for nor owned for any reason?

14. Have you ever manipulated someone into giving you something you wanted that they didn't want to give away?

15. Have you ever fantasized about committing a crime?

16. Have you ever watched people getting naked through their window?

17. Did someone else ever buy you alcohol because you were too young to buy it for yourself?

18. Did you ever take money from your mother's purse?

19. Did you ever steal something out of a sibling's closet and not give it back?

20. Did you ever kill a pet fish for fun?

21. Have you ever started a fire of any size and enjoyed it?

22. Have you ever received too much change from a store clerk and taken it on purpose without saying anything?

23. Did you ever forge your own tardy or absence note for school, work, or summer camp?

24. Did you ever use a physical ailment to get

yourself out of gym class? (And yes, a faked period counts here, ladies.)

25. Did you ever eat grapes before you paid for them at the grocery store?

26. Have you ever served food you'd dropped on the ground without saying anything to the person/people meant to eat it?

27. Have you ever spit in the food of someone who had pissed you off?

28. Did you ever sneak outside food or drink into a movie theater or restaurant?

29. Do you know what insider trading is?

30. Have you ever left a pet or a child in the car so you could meet up with some friends at a bar or restaurant?

31. Have you ever purposely dressed as a gangster in order to intimidate people?

32. Did you ever dress in a costume to avoid being spotted by someone looking for you?

33. Have you ever stolen change out of someone else's change jar?

34. Have you ever burned up an insect with a magnifying glass?

35. Did you ever try to look down girls' shirts or blouses?

36. Did you ever look up girls' skirts or dresses?

37. Have you ever urinated outside in a public place?

38. Ever taken a shit outside in a public place?

39. Ever gone camping and intentionally left your litter because you didn't feel like packing it out?

40. Have you ever gotten a rush out of making a child cry?

41. Have you ever ridden public transportation without paying?

42. Have you ever gotten a ticket for public nudity?

43. Have you ever gotten a ticket for driving more than 15 mph over the speed limit?

44. Did you ever get a detention when you were in school for any reason?

45. Did you ever go off campus for lunch when you were in high school when you weren't allowed?

46. Did you ever cut school? (Senior Cut Day does NOT count.)

47. Did you ever spread a rumor you knew wasn't true about someone because you didn't like them?

48. Have you ever gone swimming naked in a public place where it wasn't legal to swim (like the Marin County Water Supply)?

49. Have you ever keyed anyone's car because they took your parking place?

50. Have you ever gotten off at an exit because you were chasing someone who cut you off in traffic?

51. Have you ever rolled down your window and screamed obscenities at a stranger due to road rage?

52. Have you ever prayed fervently for severe harm to come to someone you didn't like?

53. Have you ever destroyed someone else's property because they pissed you off?

54. Did you ever do anyone's homework for pay?

55. Or have you ever paid anyone to do your homework?

56. Did you ever get bullied into doing someone's homework?

57. Have you ever taken something that wasn't yours and then pretended you'd just found it?

58. Have you ever held anyone underwater for so long that when they came up they were coughing?

59. Have you ever stolen your parents' car?

60. Have you ever toilet papered a neighbor's house?

61. Have you ever toilet papered someone's house that you were mad at?

62. Have you ever thrown eggs at passing trains?

63. Have you ever played poker?

64. Have you ever hustled anyone in a pool game?

65. Have you ever cheated in a game against a friend or family member?

66. Have you ever cheated during a game you were paid to play?

67. Have you ever not picked up shit after the dog you were walking left it on the sidewalk?

68. Have you ever been pulled over for driving erratically?

69. Have you ever gone through a sobriety test with a police office after being pulled over?

70. Have you ever gotten a ticket for urinating in a public place?

71. Have you ever made more than ten calls to your ex in one night?

72. Have you ever called the person you were dating to check up on them because you were jealous?

73. Have you ever driven by your boyfriend or girlfriend's house to check up on them even when you had no reason to be in their neighborhood?

74. How about the house of an ex?

75. Ever followed someone you had a crush on to see where they were going?

76. Ever secretly watched them through a window?

77. Have you ever tipped a cow?

Joselin Linder

78. Ever gone with people to tip cows even if you did not participate?

79. Do you ever have to ask yourself if something you are doing is legal or illegal?

80. Do you ever get a rush from successfully breaking the law without getting caught?

81. Have you ever thrown eggs at passing cars?

82. Have you ever rung someone's doorbell and then run away?

83. Have you ever egged someone's house?

84. Have you ever played your music so loud in your apartment that a neighbor came by to ask you to turn it off?

85. Ever have the cops show up to your house because you were being too loud?

86. Ever have the cops show up to a party you threw while your parents were out when you were a minor?

87. Have you ever played poker for money?

88. Have you ever gambled on sports?

89. Have you ever thrown a game you were playing because you had bet against yourself or were going to get a payoff?

90. Have you ever cheated in a game against a stranger?

91. Did you ever use a fake ID to get into a bar?

92. Did you ever drive a car before you had a license or a permit?

93. Did you ever use a fake ID to avoid getting in trouble for a speeding ticket?

94. Did you ever pretend not to have ID when you actually did because you were somewhere you should not have been?

95. Did you ever leave a tour group to go off exploring on your own?

96. Have you ever stolen a magazine that arrived for your neighbor?

97. Have you ever gone through all the closets and drawers at someone else's home?

98. Have you ever stolen some small souvenir from a home you were visiting?

99. Have you ever babysat and invited a friend over after the kids went to sleep?

100. Have you ever picked a flower out of a neighbor's garden without asking?

101. Have you ever picked a veggie or two out of a neighbor's garden without asking?

102. Have you ever graffitied or tagged a wall or public place?

103. Have you ever sworn at a teacher or school official?

104. Have you ever made up any "yo' mama" jokes?

105. Have you ever peed in an elevator?

106. Have you ever complained at a restaurant in order to get a free meal?

107. Have you ever made a big deal about an airline situation just to see what you could get for free out of it?

108. Have you ever ridden a motorcycle and slicked back your hair to look cool?

109. Have you ever left burning shit on anyone's doorstep?

110. Have you ever poured a whole bowl of candy into your trick-or-treat bag left by someone expecting you to use the honor system and only take one?

111. Have you ever bought scalped tickets?

112. Have you ever lied to a parent on behalf of your sibling?

113. Have you ever lied to your friend's parent on their behalf?

114. Did you ever accidentally injure or kill a family member?

115. Did you ever try to rob a bum?

116. Have you ever brandished a weapon to warn someone not to fuck with you?

117. Have you ever offered money for sex to a stranger you saw walking down the street, even in jest?

118. Have you been in a riot?

119. Has your gang ever been in a dance-off?

120. Have you ever paid a hooker for sex?

121. Have you ever taken anything from a store worth more than twenty dollars?

122. Did you ever steal from your place of employment?

123. Have you ever lied to the police?

124. Have you ever stolen a plant from a national forest?

125. Ever smuggled plants or fruits into California?

126. Have you ever lied about being sick so that you could be around someone's newborn who would not have wanted you around if they'd known?

127. Have you ever cased a joint?

128. Have you ever told the host at a busy restaurant you were diabetic, hypoglycemic, or pregnant to skip the line and get seated right away?

129. Have you ever planned a crime with someone else?

130. Have you ever skateboarded illegally?

131. Have you ever kicked a customer out of your place of employment just because you didn't like the way they looked?

132. Have you ever dined and dashed?

133. Have you dined and dashed more than once?

134. Have you ever participated in a rap-off?

135. Have you ever bought alcohol for minors?

136. Did you ever take your mom or dad's credit card and buy anything with it, then put it back without ever telling them?

137. Have you ever intentionally kicked an animal?

138. Have you ever burned something just for the sake of watching it burn?

139. Have you ever stolen from an ATM?

140. Did you ever switch tags on clothing items to get them for cheaper?

141. Would you agree with the following statement: "Everything you eat at the grocery store is free until you get to the checkout. Then you only have to pay for whatever you didn't get around to eating"?

142. Have you ever stolen a computer from a school?

143. How about an entire cash register from a business?

144. Have you ever sat in a class you didn't pay for?

145. Have you ever stolen art supplies from a classroom?

146. Ever taken more than one newspaper out of a newspaper vending machine?

147. Ever stolen books from a library?

148. Ever taken supplies from the supply cabinet at your place of employment?

149. Ever stolen toilet paper from public restrooms?

150. A towel from a hotel?

151. Have you ever stolen holiday decorations from a store?

152. How about from someone's yard?

153. Did your father ever teach you how to commit a crime?

154. Did you ever see your mother lie to get out of a speeding ticket?

155. Did you ever try to outrun a cop chasing you for speeding?

156. Did you ever get into trouble for truancy?

157. Have you ever visited anyone in juvvie?

158. Ever visited anyone in prison?

159. Did you see the inside of a courtroom as a defendant before the age of twelve?

160. How about after eighteen?

161. Have you ever thrown punches at a stranger because of road rage?

162. Have you ever let someone with road rage tailgate you and then slam on your breaks?

163. Have you ever plotted anyone's murder because you didn't like them?

Joselin Linder

164. Have you ever injured anyone's pet because you were angry at its owner?

165. Have you ever lied on your own behalf in court?

166. Did you ever bully a sibling into doing your chores when you were a kid?

167. Did you ever bully kids at your school into giving you money?

168. Has a child you were supposed to be watching ever been injured because you were talking on the phone, napping, or otherwise ignoring them?

169. Have you ever been a part of a drag race?

170. Have you ever stolen your neighbor's car?

171. Have you ever kicked or shaken a vending machine until it gave you free candy or soda?

172. Have you ever stolen the money out of a vending machine?

173. Have you ever stolen ingredients from a restaurant you worked at for a meal you planned to prepare at home?

174. Have you ever made you and your friends a huge meal at a restaurant you worked at after it had closed and the manager had left?

175. Have you ever snuck into a concert through a back door?

176. Have you ever snuck into a drive-in movie?

177. Ever stayed at a theater after watching one movie to watch another?

178. Have you ever known that someone committed a crime and not said anything?

179. Did you ever catch your parents participating in criminal activities?

180. Have you ever had information about someone else's participation in a crime and not said anything about knowing, even when asked?

181. Have you ever stolen items from a store and then returned them later for cash?

182. Have you ever counted cards while gambling?

183. Did you ever own a pet, like a large dog or a piranha, in the hopes it would intimidate people?

184. Have you ever struck either of your parents?

185. Have you ever paid anyone to hurt someone for you?

186. Have you ever sold something you'd stolen?

187. Have you ever committed statutory rape?

188. Have you ever trapped an insect in a microwave and turned it on out of morbid curiosity?

189. Have you ever not paid your rent and then insisted that you'd paid it to the landlord?

190. Have you ever been paid twice for doing a job and kept the money?

191. Have you ever gotten a child to lie to strangers for money that you then split with them?

192. Have you ever streaked?

193. Have you ever mooned or flashed anyone?

194. Have you ever hired an escort?

195. Have you ever knowingly bought anything off the black market?

196. Have you ever graffitied just to piss people off?

197. Have you ever pulled a weapon on a teacher or a school administrator?

198. Have you ever insulted somebody's mother to their face?

199. Have you ever made prank phone calls?

200. Have you ever taught a class on a subject about which you knew nothing, and made up information as you went along?

201. Have you ever knowingly overcharged anyone for services you provided?

202. Have you ever stiffed anyone for services rendered by claiming you didn't like the job they'd done?

203. Have you ever complained about a haircut so you wouldn't have to pay for it?

204. Ever complained about a spa treatment so that you could get another one for free?

205. Ever slipped in a side entrance at a movie theater so you wouldn't have to pay?

206. Have you ever blackmailed or bribed a teacher for a better grade?

207. Ever told a telemarketer that the person they were trying to reach had died in order to get them to leave you alone?

208. Have you ever flipped out on a telemarketer and called them swear words until they hung up?

209. Have you ever actually tried to hunt down a telemarketer for some face time?

210. Have you ever hacked into someone's secure system just to see if you could?

211. Have you ever scalped tickets?

212. Have you ever snuck into a classroom when no one was around and snooped through your classmates' desks and bags?

213. Did you ever cut school to go swimming because it was really hot outside?

214. Did you ever cut school to go to the mall?

215. Did you ever sell Girl Scout cookies and keep the money and fail to deliver the cookies?

216. Did you ever collect money for a charity and never hand in the funds you collected?

217. Did you ever collect money for a paper route and fail to hand over the money to the newspaper?

218. Did you ever distract a teacher or school official so someone else could sneak out of the room?

219. Have you ever left something at the scene of a crime you were committing that had your name on it or some other undeniable proof of your presence there?

220. Have you ever panicked during a crime so that you were unable to complete your mission?

221. Have you ever won a foot or bike race by taking a shortcut or sneaking a ride in a car?

222. Have you ever dressed in all black to pull off a night caper?

223. Have you ever broken into the pool of a stranger so you could go swimming?

224. Have you ever committed a crime to protest animal cruelty?

225. Have you ever committed a crime in order to rally for political change?

226. Have you ever committed a crime in protest of a political policy?

227. Are you currently on the run from the law?

228. Do you have outstanding parking tickets from a city you no longer live in?

229. Have you ever been shot by someone you were shooting at?

230. Have you ever been in a rumble?

231. Have you ever looted anything during a riot?

232. Has anyone ever pulled a switchblade on you?

233. Have you ever hooked out on the street?

234. Did you ever frame a coworker for a mistake at work because you didn't like them and wanted them fired?

235. Have you ever lied to a school administrator to avoid punishment?

236. Did you ever switch drivers at the scene of a car accident because the driver should not have been driving in the first place?

237. Have you ever broken into your parent's home to steal valuables?

238. How about the home of a friend?

239. Do you know off the top of your head how to pick a lock?

240. Can you hot-wire a car?

241. Have you ever committed a robbery with a gun?

242. Have you ever taken more than your share of something stolen? (In other words, have you ever stiffed your partner in crime?)

243. Have you ever injured anyone during a crime (either on purpose or not)?

244. Did you ever steal anyone's credit card number?

245. Ever sold drugs?

246. Have you ever purposely injured or experimented on a wild animal after trapping it?

247. Have you ever set a house on fire?

248. Have you ever set an animal on fire?

249. Did you ever cheat or try to cheat on a drug test by using an over-the-counter herbal supplement meant to mask traces of THC in your urine?

250. Did you ever cheat on a drug test by swapping your pee with someone else's clean urine?

251. Have you ever jaywalked?

252. Have you ever badly injured or even killed a stray cat?

253. Have you ever had a restraining order against you?

254. Have you ever stolen from a church collection plate?

255. Have you ever had your license suspended?

256. Have you ever traveled on someone else's passport on purpose?

257. Have you ever taken anything from a landmark or tourist attraction when no one was looking?

258. Have you ever stolen a package meant for your neighbor?

259. Have you ever babysat and invited a boyfriend/girlfriend after the kids had gone to sleep?

260. Have you ever "borrowed" a lawn mower or other gardening tool from a neighbor without asking?

261. Were you ever in juvvie long enough to hang pictures on a wall?

262. How about prison?

263. Have you ever injured anyone, even superficially, for pissing you off?

264. Have you ever tapped your car into someone else's car because they cut you off in traffic?

265. Have you ever created a false identity online and made someone fall in love with you in order to get them back for having done you wrong?

266. Have you ever created a false identity online to make someone fall in love with you so that you could steal from them?

267. Have you ever committed tax fraud?

268. Have you ever started a fake business to cover up an illegal way you were making money?

269. Have you ever run your money intentionally through the washing machine to clean it?

270. Have you ever robbed a bank?

271. Have you ever lied on someone else's behalf to a teacher?

272. How about to a school administrator?

273. Ever lied to a judge to get someone off the hook for a crime you knew they committed?

274. Did you ever physically bully anyone during

your school days, for example, by shoving them in lockers or giving them swirlies in the toilet?

275. Did you ever hit your boyfriend/girlfriend hard enough to leave a mark?

276. Did you ever beat anyone hard enough to send them to the hospital?

277. Have you ever dissected a living creature for pleasure?

278. Have you ever stolen money out of the purse of a friend or loved one?

279. Have you ever embezzled money from a corporation?

280. Have you threatened bodily harm on someone to get money from them?

281. Have you ever trespassed on private property that had a blatant NO TRESPASSING sign?

282. Ever gone swimming in the pool of a private club without being a member or a guest of a member?

283. Have you ever claimed research you found in a book as your own?

284. Have you ever plagiarized published work for a paper you were writing?

285. Have you ever stolen good quotes, tweaked them, and then claimed ownership of them?

286. Have you ever won an amateur poetry contest with a poem you did not write?

287. Have you ever tried to re-create a great piece of art to resell for a fortune?

288. Have you ever lied while in office?

289. Have you ever bought a knockoff watch on the street?

290. Ever bought a pirated movie?

291. Have you ever been physically violent with a lover out of jealousy?

292. Have you ever thrown anything at anyone during a disagreement?

293. Have you ever verbally abused a loved one and then later on tried to justify the behavior by saying they deserved it?

294. How about with physical abuse? Ever hit someone and then at a later time, said that they deserved it?

295. Have you ever stolen anything out of the home of a neighbor?

296. Have you ever seriously considered becoming a pirate?

297. Have you ever thrown rocks or stones at passing cars?

298. Have you ever thrown something as big as, or bigger than (and including) a frozen chicken at a moving vehicle?

299. Have you ever played Russian roulette?

300. Have you ever played for or worked for a sports team that you gambled against?

301. Have you ever cheated in a game you were playing professionally?

302. Have you ever lied or stolen in order to save a failing business?

303. Have you ever beaten up a homeless person?

304. Have you ever followed someone you were dating for a full day to check up on them?

305. Have you ever been arrested for stalking?

306. Have you ever participated in a "sit-in"?

307. Have you ever gone to confession or participated in some similar religious cleansing of your soul only to continue criminal or even dishonest behavior?

308. Have you ever gambled away more than a hundred dollars in one night?

309. Have you ever lost your car to gambling?

310. Do you know how to play most games you can find at a casino?

311. Did you ever drive a car after your license was suspended?

312. Have you ever gone through your neighbor's mail around the holidays looking for cash in the greeting cards?

313. Do you plan to now that the idea has been presented to you?

314. Have you ever babysat and left the kids alone while you went out for a little while?

315. Have you ever been forced to do something immoral by a boss or lover?

316. Have you ever spied on anyone?

317. Have you ever broken into a summer home left vacant for the winter?

318. Have you ever graffitied or tagged in a cemetery?

319. Have you ever desecrated a sacred place?

320. Have you ever danced on the grave of someone you hated?

321. Have you ever been punched for insulting somebody's mother?

322. Have you ever killed anyone for having information that could get you into a lot of trouble?

323. Have you ever threatened anyone with bodily injury if they didn't leave town?

324. Ever been threatened and had to go into any kind of hiding?

325. Have you ever robbed a convenience store?

326. Have you ever stolen a purse from an old woman?

327. Ever taken candy from a baby?

328. Have you ever picked a fight with someone for no good reason?

329. Have you ever gotten involved in a fight started by a friend for no good reason?

330. Did you ever watch someone get beaten and not intervene?

331. Have you ever trained a dog to bite other people?

332. Have you ever squatted in an apartment until they evicted you?

333. Have you ever harmed or injured anyone to get into a gang or club?

334. Have you ever committed a serial crime to see how long you could get away with it?

335. Did you ever take advantage of a natural disaster to steal things?

336. Have you ever hacked into a government system and sold information to our enemies?

337. Did you ever ask someone who loved you to lie for you, like your mom or lover to get you out of a punishment?

338. Did you ever participate in a criminal scheme that involved your entire family?

339. Did you ever participate in one perpetrated by the company you work for?

340. Have you ever gone camping on private property without permission?

341. Did you ever deny someone a job because you didn't want an employee of their race or ethnicity?

342. How about gender?

343. Have you ever illegally sold stock?

344. Have you ever been charged with kidnapping or could you have been if charges had been pressed?

345. Did you ever distract a cop to give someone else time to commit a crime or just wrap it up?

346. Did you ever call 911 to report a crime you committed to make you look innocent?

347. Have you ever egged a business?

348. Did you ever break a window on purpose or by accident?

349. Did you ever pretend you were in one work meeting to avoid a different one?

350. Did you ever tell a cop you were heading to the hospital to deal with an emergency to get out of a speeding ticket?

351. Have you ever struck either of your grandparents?

352. Have you ever struck a child?

353. Have you ever left a pet outside for more than twelve hours in either dead winter or midsummer

because you couldn't be bothered to let them in or were otherwise selfishly occupied?

354. Have you ever had a job working with the elderly where you stole from them?

355. Have you ever organized a phone scam to trick people into giving you money?

356. Have you ever stolen anyone's identity for monetary gain?

357. Have you ever trapped or tried to trap a groundhog or some other burrowing animal in its hole and then filled it with water?

358. Have you ever stolen a baby Jesus from a nativity scene?

359. Have you ever been ticketed or arrested for public indecency?

360. Have you ever been ticketed for having sex in public?

361. Have you ever stolen anything from someone's house where you were a guest at a party?

362. Have you ever "shared" an all-you-can-eat breakfast/salad bar?

363. Have you ever been in a bar fight?

364. Have you ever flicked off another driver in a fit of road rage?

365. Have you ever stolen money from your partner?

366. Have you ever gone behind a bar and made yourself a drink while the bartender was away?

367. Have you ever pickpocketed?

368. Have you ever driven a car without a legal driver's license?

369. Have you ever sucked on a penny to mask the smell of booze on your breath?

370. Have you ever driven drunk?

371. Have you ever kept money you found in a wallet even though the information about the owner was on the driver's license?

372. Have you ever sought revenge on someone that was acquitted of a crime you believe them to have committed?

373. Have you ever taken a hostage?

374. Have you ever tried to shoot the president?

375. Have you ever tried to car bomb a political figure?

376. Have you ever been investigated by the FBI or the CIA for some Internet or cell phone dialogue you had?

377. Have you ever damaged a parked car and driven away without leaving a note?

378. Ever hit an animal with your car and then not pull over to assess the damages incurred by the animal?

379. Do you know how to build a bomb?

380. Have you ever done research on how to poison someone?

381. Have you ever blackmailed someone for money because you knew they had done something that was embarrassing?

382. Ever done anything desperate to keep a job, like blackmail an employer?

383. Have you ever paid someone off in order to keep them from getting you in trouble with information they had about you that you didn't want getting out?

384. Ever slept with someone so that later on you could extort money from them?

385. Have you ever participated in a crime and then used what you knew to get others in trouble?

386. How about to save yourself after everyone was found out?

387. Have you ever left your car in slow-moving traffic because it was faster to walk and gone back for it later?

388. Have you ever stolen anything from a friend's home when you were left alone for any length of time?

389. Have you ever downloaded a movie from the Internet illegally?

390. Ever shown a movie to a roomful of people as

The Purity Test

a means of making money without acquiring the rights?

391. Ever bought a knockoff bag or purse?

392. Have you ever taken pictures in an art museum or someplace else where photography was off limits?

393. Have you ever recorded a rock show on a recorder you smuggled into the venue?

394. Did you then sell the tapes?

395. Ever videotaped a movie in a movie theater?

396. Have you ever injured an animal in the making of a movie and then put the statement in the credits that no animal was injured in the making of it?

397. Have you ever claimed a coat at a coat check that was not yours because you liked it better than your own?

398. Have you ever intentionally killed a stranger?

399. Have you ever intentionally killed a friend?

400. Is it possible that these questions might finally make you snap?

YOUR CRIMINAL BEHAVIOR PURITY NUMBER:
_____%

The Cardinal Vice Purity Test

If it's vain, gluttonous, envious, wrathful, lustful, greedy, prideful, sneezy, or Doc, you'll find it here in the Cardinal Vice Purity section. The cardinal vices, otherwise known as the Seven Deadly Sins, were originally used in early Christian teachings because people did all kinds of fucked-up shit back then and the church needed some quick and dirty tips for saving your soul, a sort of Bill of Rights to the Ten Commandments' Constitution.

The questions in this section may not all seem steeped in holiness. Just understand that they maintain a holy spirit. In other words, just because you are not asked if you said a prayer before you ate the whole cake but are instead asked if you ate a whole cake, alone, in one sitting, before the previews were even over, what you are being asked about are your gluttonous tendencies, not how skillfully you can pray and do the soft shoe at the same time.

In case you've never lit the Sabbath candles, bowed in the direction of Mecca, but you have been burned by holy water, here is a rundown of those Seven Deadly Sins. For you goody two-shoes, we'll match them with the Seven Holy Virtues.

Lust We're all familiar with sexual lust, but when it comes to sin, lust is really any uncontrolled desire. Bloodlust. Lust for power. Lust is a desire so deep and so twisted, you'll risk it all for a taste of what you want. Sort of like that craving you get for McDonald's french fries when you're really drunk, but times ten. And instead of french fries, it's fucking your boss's wife.

Chastity Don't have sex before marriage. Why? Oh, right, so you don't find out about your husband's back hair and raging herpes sores until your magical wedding night. Surprise!

Gluttony You're standing at the all-you-can-eat "salad" bar at Ponderosa, ogling everything from the fried chicken to the chocolate Jell-O. Then you start to feel guilty about your impending overindulgence. "What's so wrong with this?" you ask. "Even the wontons look fresh!" But it *is* wrong. Not because of the pickled pigs' feet (although they are also wrong), but because NO ONE SHOULD EVER EAT ALL THEY CAN! Gluttony will send you to hell in the end, but on the bright side, it's yummy!

Temperance Knowing when to say when and confidently staring temptation in the face. Temperance can be uncomfortable while you're going through heroin withdrawal, but mostly because you'll be shitting yourself. Later on, you'll be glad you kicked the habit.

Greed As Gordon Gekko remarked in the immortal film *Wall Street*, greed is good. Here in America, sharing is for suckers and commies. It's winner-take-all and to hell with second place. Unfortunately, what's good for the USA is bad for the fate of your everlasting soul, so if avarice is your vice, savor your wealth while you can and prepare to spend eternity as a camel trying to squeeze through the eye of a needle.

Charity Pretty much exclusively for suckers and commies.

Sloth You know when you skip making the bed because you're only going to sleep in it again the next night? That's sloth. Kicking back, taking it easy, going the slow and easy route. Sure, you could get that report done on time, but life's too short to spend scurrying from deadline to deadline. If your boss doesn't like it, well, you're going to tell that bastard off as soon as you wake up from a little snooze. But after that you're really going to let that son of a zzzzzzzzzzzz . . .

Diligence The compulsion to keep busy and never stop working. The thing about diligence as opposed to sloth is that sleep isn't a necessity—the only necessity is success. A heart attack at forty is God's way of saying keep up the good work and you'll get to heaven in half the time!

Wrath The Old Testament is full of angry God, vengeful God, burning-bush God. But Jesus put the kibosh on wrath with his cheek-turning policies, so the next time that little brat of yours runs his mouth off, instead of giving him a fat lip, throw on a meditation tape and stuff your rage deep, deep down in your psyche where it will manifest itself as high blood pressure and an early grave. Once again, think of it as a shortcut to eternal paradise.

Forgiveness The next time someone says they're sorry for anything—like crossing the median drunk and smashing into your new car with their pickup truck—smile with the teeth you have left and embrace them in a very convincing hug. Then punch them in the face. Then apologize. That way you can both reap the holy benefits of forgiveness.

Envy Remember how that girl with the big horsy teeth got really hot after your buddy started dating her? Did she always have that ass? Everything looks better when someone else has it, which is yet another way that God makes sure that nobody's happy.

Kindness People say that a little kindness goes a long way. So keep it to a minimum and you should do just fine.

Pride This is a tricky sin. The minute you manage to stop feeling pride in your accomplishments, you congratulate yourself for conquering pride and end up right back where you started. It's Sisyphean.

Humility You're humble, huh? Well, congratulations. You realize that by even letting your humility be known you're killing your humility score. You need to be so

Richard the Purity Gerbil says:

This is the cardinal purity section, which means it's time to pay the piper for a lifetime of deadly sins.

You can bet your wings the guys upstairs are on to you. If you want to see how thirsty you oughta be for a pint of foaming holy water, take this test as seriously as a crucifixion. *Capisce?*

The commandments of this section include: When coming across a question like "Have you ever eaten an entire meal in front of a starving homeless person?" and you think, "I've eaten a whole ice cream sundae with extra whip *off* a starving homeless person," or something similar, you can give yourself a *yes* based on the "Or Something Similar" clause.

Scores for this section are as easy to obtain as an icy beer out of the beer fridge of Satan's air-conditioned pool hall. (Yeah, right):

- Keep track of your *no* answers.
- Divide your total after 400 questions by 4.
- Drop any decimals or remainders.
- Add a percentage.
- *Example: 290 no answers divided by 4 is 72.5, which makes your Purity Number 72 percent.*

humble nobody even knows you're humble, so you can't even get credit for that.

1. Are you your favorite topic of conversation?

2. Have you ever eaten an entire bag of potato chips (not the individual-size bags) in one sitting?

3. Have you ever played an online game for longer than three hours straight?

4. Have you ever lied to someone you are sleeping with about having an STD? (Not telling them you have one is lying.)

5. Have you ever lied to a doctor about a medical condition because you felt embarrassed?

6. Have you ever stayed in a relationship you hated because you didn't think the person could handle it if you broke up with them?

7. Do you not have a baby or a pet because you think you are just too selfish right now?

8. Do you figure you will remain selfish for the foreseeable future?

9. Have you ever photographed your own genitals?

10. Ever kill a pet fish because you were tired of taking care of it?

11. Have you ever tricked someone into looking stupid because you were jealous of how smart they were?

12. Do you have a particular dislike for people who can do your job better than you?

13. Do you generally hate people who are pretty and know it?

14. Have you ever sat someone down and told them things you didn't like about them to get it off your chest?

15. Have you ever been purposely mean to someone because you were jealous of the way they looked?

16. Have you ever tried to trip someone or otherwise get an advantage in a sporting event?

17. Ever tried to break the legs of an athletic rival?

18. Have you ever taken an article of clothing from someone?

19. Have you ever pretended to be someone you were jealous of?

20. Have you ever done anything mean to someone whom you believed your significant other might be attracted to? (The answer is still *yes* even if you were right and they left you for them!)

21. Do you figure if you'd been given the opportunity you could have been the first to break the sound barrier or go into space?

22. Would you pose naked for one thousand dollars?

23. How about ten thousand dollars?

24. Would you do it for free as long as it would help your career?

25. Have you ever written your own memoirs because you can't imagine a life more worthy of going down on paper?

26. Ever worn a corset to make you look skinnier?

27. Ever worn a girdle to tighten your ass?

28. Ever complained about not having been given enough alcohol in your cocktail?

29. How about portion size? Ever argued that a restaurant didn't serve you enough food?

30. Have you ever watched a reality show marathon through more than two episodes in one sitting?

31. Have you ever burned old furniture because you didn't know what else to do with it?

32. Have you ever thrown garbage into a lake or river or ocean because you didn't feel like taking it with you off the boat or dock?

33. Have you ever left a faucet running all night?

34. Do you think that you are better than others because of your religion?

35. Have you ever bought more than three hundred dollars worth of clothes without trying them on first?

36. Do you think you are your parents' favorite child?

37. Do you believe you are generally the dumbest person in the room?

38. Do you figure that it is inevitable that you will end up alone and deeply in debt?

39. Do you think you could figure out how to fly without an airplane if you had enough time, money, and resources?

40. Do you think you'd make a really good dictator?

41. Have you ever been injured in a game you, in retrospect, were not qualified to be playing?

42. Have you ever slept until sundown?

43. Have you ever slept for at least twenty-four hours?

44. Have you ever played a computer game until the sun came up?

45. Have you ever masturbated in the bathroom of a strip club?

46. Have you ever skipped work to play a video game?

47. Have you ever skipped work to sleep?

48. Have you ever skipped work to spend time with a friend or significant other?

49. Do you believe you are the best person in the whole world?

50. Do you ever eat more of something just because it tastes good and not because you are hungry?

51. Have you ever bought something you wanted in more than one color because you couldn't decide?

52. Have you ever ordered more than one dinner at a restaurant because you weren't sure what you wanted?

53. Have you ever eaten the leftovers of everyone at the table after lunch or dinner?

54. Have you ever ordered all the desserts on a menu?

55. Have you ever eaten more than one box of candy during one movie?

56. Have you ever scratched a mosquito bite until it bled?

57. Have you ever gone to a movie theater to watch porn?

58. Have you ever gotten a score higher than 100,000 on Ms. Pac-Man?

59. Do you think you are the most hardworking person at your office?

60. Do you have any piercings other than in your earlobes?

61. Have you ever walked into a party thinking about how hot you looked?

62. Have you ever called yourself beautiful or hot in front of other people and meant it?

63. Have you ever looked in the mirror at yourself naked and considered how great you looked?

64. Have you ever spent a whole day doing things to make yourself beautiful (like a facial and a manicure)?

65. Do you ever think about how brilliant you sound during conversations?

66. Do you think you give fantastic advice?

67. Do you think people are always looking at you when you are in public?

68. Have you ever been in a conversation where you clearly talked more than the other person?

69. Do you ever have conversations and think about what a moron the person is to whom you are talking?

70. Do you enjoy talking about your friends behind their backs?

71. Are you ever nice to people to their faces even when you dislike them?

72. Do you think you were probably the best artist in your kindergarten class?

73. Do you think your kids or nieces and nephews are or will be the smartest in their classes?

74. Do you think your kids or nieces and nephews are or will be the best looking in their school?

75. Do you think your kids or nieces and nephews are or will be the best athletes on their teams?

76. Do you have a specific dislike for people from a city that has a sports team that rivals one you like?

77. Do you think you are your grandparents' favorite grandchild?

78. Have you ever given a gift you received to someone else as a gift (regifting)?

79. Have you ever gotten your own dinner and refused to share it at a meal where everyone else was sharing (like at a Chinese restaurant)?

80. Have you ever told someone they smelled bad (even if they really did smell bad)?

81. Have you ever promised something and then found yourself unable to deliver?

82. Have you ever been injured because you overestimated your abilities?

83. Have you ever played chicken in a car?

84. Have you ever finished a pint of ice cream in one sitting?

85. How about a gallon?

86. Have you ever roasted a pig on a spit and eaten it?

87. Have you ever eaten a whole can of Spam by yourself in one sitting?

88. Have you ever eaten peanut butter and or jelly out of the jar?

89. Have you ever eaten raw sugar out of a bag of sugar?

90. Have you ever eaten dog food?

91. Have you ever eaten the food leftover by strangers at a restaurant table?

92. Ever asked at a restaurant for extra bread in your doggie bag even though you'd already eaten the bread that they had brought to the table?

93. Have you ever finished orphaned cans or bottles of beer at a party?

94. How about at a bar?

95. Have you ever been out with you, your significant other, and another couple and found your partner severely lacking?

96. Have you ever wished your partner was more like your parent or sibling?

97. How about a good friend's partner? Ever wished you could swap your boyfriend/girlfriend for theirs?

98. Ever found a good friend's partner revolting?

99. Have you ever followed the rules in a book to get someone to fall for you?

100. Have you ever drank heavy cream out of the carton?

101. Have you ever swallowed a live goldfish?

102. Have you ever peed in a swimming pool?

103. Have you ever read a pop culture magazine from cover to cover?

104. Have you ever gossiped about a celebrity?

105. Have you ever enjoyed listening to gossip about celebrities?

106. Have you ever made up gossip about a celebrity for the sake of conversation?

107. Have you ever put a different cover on a book you were reading to make people around you think you were reading something different than you actually were?

108. Have you ever put a news magazine under a smut magazine so no one would know what you were reading?

109. Have you ever memorized a few facts about something you otherwise knew nothing about in order to sound like an expert in a social situation?

110. Do you ever wear an outfit and carry yourself in a way that makes you seem wealthier than you actually are?

111. Have you ever taken someone out on a date and spent far more than you could actually afford in order to impress them?

112. Have you ever lied to your parents about how much money you are making?

113. Would you beat someone up for insulting your mother?

114. Have you ever eaten a stick of butter by itself in one sitting?

115. How about on bread? Ever polished off a whole stick on bread in one go?

116. Have you ever eaten bread fried in bacon grease?

117. Have you ever had to unbutton your pants while eating a big meal?

118. Ever drank out of a straw so you wouldn't mess up your lipstick?

119. Did you ever wear colored contacts and try to pass them off as your actual eye color?

120. Did you ever wear invisible braces?

121. Have you ever eaten until you were full, burped, and continued eating?

122. Have you ever eaten until you were full, taken a nap, and continued eating?

123. Have you ever eaten ice cream with your fingers?

124. Have you ever illegally smuggled any foodstuff over international borders? (For example, it is illegal to import cheese or meat into the United States without declaring it on international flights.)

125. Do you believe stealing is a breach of divine law?

126. Do you hope all criminals will burn in an actual Hell or something similar?

127. Do you believe that people in general are so bad that you hope Hell is as uncomfortable as they say—maybe more so?

128. Have you ever had an incredibly rich fantasy life with a celebrity you had never met?

129. Did you ever hang more than two pictures of any one celebrity on your wall at one time?

130. Did you ever join a celebrity fan club with the expectation that you would actually get to meet that person?

131. Have you ever lost weight to try and impress someone?

132. Have you ever gained weight because your partner asked you to?

133. Have you ever skipped church to watch a football game?

134. Ever skipped an important meeting because you were scared to show up?

135. Have you ever lied about the health of your parents to avoid doing something else?

136. Ever claimed to be going to the funeral of your grandparents to get out of any other function?

137. Have you ever told your office you missed your flight in order to extend your vacation by another day?

138. Ever called in sick when you felt fantastic?

139. Have you ever called your kid's school and said they were sick to get them out of taking a test they weren't prepared for?

140. Have you ever lied about your car breaking down to explain why you were late?

141. Have you ever eaten a dog biscuit?

142. Have you ever eaten a hotdog or hamburger that you were cooking over an open fire that had fallen into the flames and was covered in ash because you were really hungry?

143. Have you ever been hungry enough to eat raw pasta?

144. Have you ever eaten raw meat?

145. Have you ever had Botox injections?

146. Have you ever had liposuction?

147. Ever had a tummy tuck or your stomach stapled to limit your eating?

148. Ever joined Weight Watchers or Jenny Craig?

149. Have you ever had laser surgery on your eyes so that you wouldn't have to wear glasses?

150. Ever had a nose job?

151. Have you ever encouraged anyone to have a boob job?

152. Have you ever wished you had bigger or smaller boobs or wished it of your partner?

153. Ever wished you had a bigger or smaller penis or wished it of your partner?

154. Ever wished you had fuller lips?

155. How about a bigger or smaller ass?

156. Have you ever wished you were shorter or taller than you are?

157. Have you ever paid for someone else's plastic surgery?

158. Have you ever agreed to volunteer someplace and then backed out at the last minute?

159. Have you ever taught a person to read incorrectly?

160. Have you ever agreed to give money to a charity and then not gotten around to paying it?

161. Have you ever thought of a great idea for a nonprofit organization or NGO but done nothing to help make it a reality?

162. Are you completely unaware of the number of paper products you dispose of every day?

163. Do you drink more than five disposable bottles of water per week?

164. Do you fill up your gas tank more than once a week?

165. Do you carpool?

166. Do you brush your teeth fewer than two times a day?

167. Do you refuse to eat leftovers?

168. Do you eat out more than ten times per week?

169. Are you completely clueless about how long it takes to hard-boil an egg?

170. Did you get your own car on your sixteenth birthday?

171. Have your parents ever bought you a car?

172. Have your parents ever bought you a home?

173. Have you ever cleaned your own toilet (including the crusty nast under the seat)?

174. Were you ever on a cruise before the age of ten?

175. Have you ever tried to get into the FBI and failed?

176. Have you ever tried to get into the NASA program and failed?

177. Have you ever come up with ideas for the military that you believe they need in order to win the war on terrorism and done nothing about it?

178. Did your grandparents die before you ever thought to ask them about their lives?

179. On a first date, do you prefer to do most of the talking?

180. Are you more interested in people who are dressed fashionably than people who don't follow trends?

181. Do you shower more than once a day?

182. Have you ever skipped down the street because you felt happy?

183. Have you ever screamed because you were so pissed off?

184. Have you ever cried because you didn't get your way?

185. Can you fake cry convincingly?

186. Have you ever jumped out of a dark corner and scared anyone?

187. Have you ever pretended to be asleep to see what people would say about you?

188. Have you ever gone into a fit of raging hysterics and needed to be restrained?

189. Have you ever said threatening and abusive things to anyone to vent general frustrations?

190. Have you ever thrown anything across the room when you lost control of your temper?

191. Did you ever genuinely mean to have a few

friends over, only to watch the whole night turn into the party of the century?

192. Did you ever blatantly disregard the wishes of your parents in order to follow selfish pursuits?

193. Did you ever spend more than a hundred dollars on a haircut?

194. Did you ever spend money on clothing you couldn't afford and didn't need?

195. Have you ever gone to a dance club and been jealous when the crowd circled up to watch someone else dance?

196. Have you ever made fun of the performance of someone who got the role in a school play that should have been yours?

197. Have you ever made fun of the athletic ability of someone who got your spot on the athletic team?

198. Have you ever been jealous of the career of a friend?

199. Ever been jealous of their love affair?

200. Ever wished you had more curves?

201. Have you ever attempted to live off-grid for any period of time?

202. Do you think the idea of adopting one night a week where you keep all your lights off and unplug all your appliances to try to live a greener life sounds like about the lamest thing you've ever heard?

203. Do you refuse to compost your rotting food?

204. Do you throw aluminum cans and glass bottles in the regular trash if you go to a restaurant that doesn't offer a recycling receptacle?

205. Does your city offer recycling whose rules you categorically refuse to follow?

206. Are you just too lazy to figure out what those rules are?

207. Have you ever been ticketed for a failure to recycle properly?

208. Do you live in a city that still does not recycle?

209. Have you ever complained about that?

210. Do you choose not to recycle if your city does not?

211. Do you feel good about using all the resources you need as long as you are comfortable?

212. Do you ever feel the need to punch hippies?

213. Do you ever use your wiles to get what you want at work?

214. Have you ever fallen for someone else using their wiles to get what they wanted at work?

215. Have you ever been sexually harassed at work?

216. Did you kind of like it?

217. Did you ever tell someone you found threatening in a work environment that you found them attractive to knock them down a peg?

218. Ever given work you were expected to do to an intern so you didn't have to bother with it?

219. Did you ever hide some alcohol for yourself at the beginning of a party for you to drink later when the rest of the booze was gone?

220. Have you ever held onto a joint for more than one hit when it was being passed around a circle to make sure you'd smoked as much as you wanted to?

221. Did you decide not to go to college?

222. Did you fail to finish college?

223. Do you think people who didn't go to college are less smart than people who did?

224. Do you think people who do drugs are evil?

225. Do you wish you lived in a different era?

226. Do you believe it is important to win no matter what is at stake?

227. Have you ever beaten a child at a child's game?

228. Have you ever worked so hard on something you ruined it?

229. Have you ever zoned out while working on an important project and ruined it?

230. Have you ever cried when you didn't win?

231. Do you still not understand how your car works (basically) even though you spend half of your life in one?

232. Do you still not understand how a computer works (basically) even though you spend most of your life on one?

233. Do you still lack a basic understanding of how your body works?

234. Have you ever listened to music you hated to impress somebody?

235. Have you ever gone to a music concert pretending to know the band you were seeing even though you had no idea who it was?

236. Did you pay out of your own pocket to see them?

237. Have you ever tried to get a kid interested in the music you like in order to guide them to what is cool?

238. Have you ever thrown a tantrum when you didn't get your way?

239. Have you ever put your fist through a wall because you were so angry?

240. Have you ever hit yourself hard enough to break or bruise the skin?

241. Have you ever broken someone's nose?

242. Have you ever punched anyone so hard they bled from someplace on their face?

243. Do you have any siblings you do not speak to even though they have asked for your forgiveness?

244. Will your parents no longer speak to you?

245. Did you live with your parents after the age of twenty-five?

246. Did you live anywhere rent free after the age of thirty?

247. Is your income whatever change you find on the street?

248. Do you think people who get paid to play video games have the best job ever?

249. Will you deny people your viable organs because you are either too lazy to make your wishes known or because you couldn't give a shit about those sick assholes? They were probably smokers anyway!

250. Do you rarely call your parents, even though they are always leaving you messages?

251. Are you too lazy to call your grandparents?

252. How about your siblings?

253. Are you pretty much only friends with the people you are friends with because they either live with you or come by all the time?

254. Do you hate people who are always organizing activities?

255. Do you think people who got married and had children right out of college must be miserable?

256. Do you think marriage is for suckers?

257. Do you hate most of your friends when they get into the gooey honeymoon phase of a new relationship?

258. Have you ever accidentally gotten pregnant or gotten someone pregnant?

259. Have you ever eaten ketchup out of the bottle?

260. Have you ever gone for seconds when you knew some people had not yet had firsts?

261. Have you ever warmed milk on the stove and had it poured in a bathtub in which you could soak?

262. Have you ever bathed in caviar?

263. Have you ever had a servant?

264. How about a housekeeper?

265. Ever hired a cleaning service?

266. Do you own anything that is twenty-four-karat gold?

267. Do you own any real diamonds?

268. Did you get your first expensive jewelry before you were eighteen?

269. Do you think a man has to buy a woman a diamond ring for their engagement to be legit?

270. Have you ever given someone something expensive, broken up with them, and then insisted they give it back?

271. Have you ever left dishes in the sink for someone else to wash?

272. Clothes in the washing machine for someone else to fold?

273. Did anyone in your favorite band die of a drug overdose?

274. Do you play your music really loud because it's so good that everyone should hear it?

275. If you were in a band would you make an amazing front man?

276. Did you decide not to go to medical school because four years seemed like too long to learn how to do things like cut flesh open and other things you've already spent a lifetime perfecting?

277. Are you pretty sure your sibling isn't yet married because he/she is a little bit in love with you?

278. Do you think if you died that certain people would just blow their own brains out, they'd be so emotionally ill-equipped to deal with the trauma?

279. Is your favorite part of recording yourself on tape going back and listening to yourself talk?

280. Do you love violent movies?

281. Have you ever made your own sex toy?

282. Do you know all the words to *The Golden Age of Grotesque*?

283. Do you kind of understand what happened at Columbine High School, at least in a *Heathers* sort of way?

284. Have you ever plotted the murders of the popular kids in your school?

285. Do you own more than one shade of red nail polish?

286. Did you ever have the same Hot Wheels in more than one color?

287. Do you always order more than one scoop of ice cream at an ice cream parlor because you can't decide on a flavor?

288. Is your partner unable to grasp their other hand when they wrap their arms around your middle?

289. Do your upper arms flap around in the breeze?

290. Do you prefer watching TV over talking to other humans?

291. Have you ever consumed an entire forty of malt liquor in full public view?

292. In private?

293. Have you ever used a whole bottle of soap in one washing?

294. Ever pretended like you were out of cigarettes because you didn't want to share?

295. Have you ever made it seem like you had less food than you actually had so you wouldn't have to give any away?

296. Did you ever ignore a pet for long periods of time because it bored you?

297. Ever had a dog you never ever took on a walk because you aren't a walker?

298. Have you ever been too tired at the end of the day to bother brushing your teeth or washing your face?

299. Have you ever shown up late to an event where your whole team is counting on you?

300. Ever failed to show up at all to an organized event where your absence meant your team had to forfeit?

301. Have you ever tried to give yourself oral sex?

302. Have you ever masturbated to avoid having to get off the highway to pee?

303. Have you ever gotten yourself off while sitting at a table with other people whom you believe had no idea about what you were doing?

304. Have you ever climbed a tree to get something down that was stuck in it, just because you wanted to look cool?

305. Did you ever try to jump off anything with a parachute made out of a sheet/blanket from your bed?

306. Did you ever try to slip your arm around someone's shoulders at the movies without them noticing?

307. Have you ever snuck into the V.I.P. section of a concert or sporting event?

308. Have you ever pushed your way to the front row of a concert?

309. Have you ever not studied for a test you had no doubt you would pass and then totally failed it?

310. Have you ever gotten every single question wrong on a test?

311. Have you ever shown up to somebody's birthday even though you weren't invited?

312. Ever spent the night on a sidewalk to be the first to buy a new CD, see a movie, or get the latest version of a video game?

313. Do you watch movies you love over and over?

314. Can you recite dialogue from a movie you have seen way too many times?

315. Have you ever bid in an auction more money than you could afford on memorabilia from a movie or TV show you were obsessed with?

316. Have you failed to write thank-you notes for most of the gifts and favors you have received in your life?

317. Have you ever opted to watch porn over going on a date with a person you figured wasn't going to put out anyway?

318. Have you ever spent an entire workday making a rubber ball out of rubber bands?

319. Have you ever jerked off with toothpaste only to realize after the fact that it really stings?

320. Have you ever fantasized about killing your own children?

321. Ever driven drunk because you lost track of how much you were drinking?

322. Have you ever sniffed your friend's mom's panties?

323. Have you ever sniffed panties you found at the Laundromat?

324. Have you ever cum into food and eaten it?

325. Have you ever cum into food and fed it to anyone?

326. Ever done it with them knowing?

327. Have you ever knowingly eaten food that had cum in it?

328. Have you ever killed a garden by forgetting to weed or water it?

329. Have you ever played footsie with someone, only to have someone you didn't expect say, "Whose foot is that?" to a table full of people?

330. Have you ever had a friend hug you platonically and put your hand very deliberately onto their not-so-platonic ass?

331. Do you pay a therapist so you can have an audience for your stories about yourself?

332. Have you ever felt disgusted by talentless people in the public eye?

333. Did you still on occasion find those same talentless people fascinating?

334. Have you ever avoided skiing or skating or any other activity because you were too scared to try?

335. Have you ever been yelled at by a pool lifeguard for standing too long on the high dive because you were too terrified to jump?

336. Ever had to end up coming down via the ladder?

337. Have you ever kept a wild animal as a pet?

338. Have you ever had more than fourteen stitches on one gash?

339. Have you ever made a Molotov cocktail?

340. Did you know any police officers in your hometown by name?

341. Have you ever gone swimming in a neighbor's pool when you knew they weren't home?

342. Did you ever sunbathe to get a good tan even though you knew it was bad for you?

343. Have you ever sunbathed nude?

344. Ever been naked on a beach with children around?

345. Have you ever traveled to a country without a

visa to which it is illegal for Americans to go without
a visa?

346. Have you ever organized a rave?

347. Have you ever gone out dressed in nothing
more than a trench coat?

348. Have you ever shut anyone inside a locker?

349. Have you ever plotted an assassination of any
president of any country?

350. Have you ever collected disability payments
even though you felt great?

351. Have you ever missed a phone call intentionally
and then later on lied and said you didn't hear your
phone to the person who'd been trying to reach you?

352. Have you ever parked in a handicap spot
using someone else's handicap stickers or tags?

353. How about without the tags?

354. Have you ever hung out shirtless at a bar or
club?

355. Have you ever worn flip-flops to a formal
dinner?

356. Have you ever burned a bra?

357. Have you ever burned anyone in effigy?

358. Have you ever made a voodoo doll?

359. Have you ever panhandled even though you
weren't that desperate for money?

360. Have you ever broken into a professional baseball field to run all the bases?

361. Have you ever dug up a grave to see the body?

362. What about to see if there was anything to steal inside the casket?

363. Do you ever groom your pubic hair?

364. Do you insist on your partner doing a thorough cleaning of their nether regions before beginning any sexual activity?

365. Have you ever competed in a tournament thinking there would be no chance of you losing and then you totally lost?

366. Ever been in a beauty pageant?

367. Ever been in a beauty pageant feeling confident in your baton twirling routine, only to have Miss Georgia beat you out with her rendition of "Ave Maria" on water goblets?

368. Have you ever tried to date a beauty queen?

369. Have you ever dated a model?

370. Are you pretty sure you could snag a model if given the opportunity?

371. Have you ever had sex with someone whom you knew thought you were someone else?

372. Ever called and hung up on a crush because you were too nervous to speak?

373. Have you ever lied about eating something

really bad for you to someone who was supposed to be helping you lose weight?

374. Ever lie about your drug use to someone who was supposed to be helping you quit?

375. Ever tell a date you thought cigarettes were a disgusting habit, all the while carrying around a pack you couldn't wait to smoke?

376. Have you ever tried going to the police for help after getting screwed over in a drug deal?

377. Ever offered a cop drugs in exchange for your freedom?

378. Have you ever had enough plastic surgery that you knew everyone knew you'd had it without your having to mention it?

379. Ever have such a great nose job or some other procedure completed that you suddenly became incredibly hot?

380. Have you ever had a plastic surgeon botch a procedure anywhere on your body?

381. Have you ever sued anyone in the medical profession?

382. Have you ever gone Dumpster diving?

383. Ever picked up furniture you saw on the street only to get it home and find out it was covered in animal urine or some insect?

384. Were you ever expelled from a school?

385. Ever gotten kicked out of an extracurricular program?

386. Have you ever claimed to have met a celebrity, even though you hadn't?

387. Have you ever claimed to have caught a really big fish that you threw back when you did not?

388. Have you ever claimed to have made a sweater you were wearing knowing full well you did not?

389. Ever claim to have made a meal from scratch that you'd ordered in?

390. How about a recipe that was not yours that you insisted was?

391. Do you think God thinks very highly of what He has done with you?

392. Do you think God is a woman?

393. Or that God lives on a mountain in Greece and has sex with virgins in the form of a bull?

394. Or that God is dead?

395. Or in the details?

396. Are you 99 percent sure God doesn't give two shits about whether or not you smoke that joint?

397. Have you spent time considering how much of your life you have wasted answering pointless questions?

398. How about now?

399. Do you think people who take this test are generally idiots?

400. Do you think the person who wrote this test is the biggest idiot of all?

> YOUR CARDINAL VICE PURITY NUMBER: _____%

Congratulations! You've finished the General Purity Test! Take your scores from all four sections, add your *no* answers, and divide by sixteen. That's your General Purity Number, and we challenge you to find a more accurate reading anywhere else.

So, you have a groove going.

Or you're completely dissatisfied.

Or you feel dirty and hope there's redemption.

Or you've been misunderstood.

If the GPT didn't fit your bill, don't worry. You haven't been forgotten. Without question, one of the following three tests will be the one for you!

The Male
Purity Test

This Purity Test measures masculinity with scientific accuracy. (And men love numbers—how else to explain the popularity of mind-numbing "fantasy baseball.") Where a somewhat masculine woman might be excused as a tomboy, a man displaying an equal degree of feminine behavior doesn't get a nice word, except maybe *fruit*. Nothing wrong with being called an orange or banana, right? Anyway, whichever team you're pitching for, masculinity is masculinity, and that pretty much boils down to beer with spicy buffalo wings, exceptionally long trips to the bathroom, football, at least three close friends commonly referred to by their last names, and without exception the ability to spit great distances.

So take the test. See where you stand. But whatever you do, don't cry about it!

Richard the Purity Gerbil says:

Guys like it short and sweet, or was it long and spicy? Either Way, here's the beef: add up your *no* answers. That's your Male Purity Number expressed as a percentage. For example: if you get 22 *no* answers, your Purity Number is 22 percent. Got it, bud? Now put on that jockstrap and saddle up.

1. Have you ever ended up dating anyone who didn't let you kiss them on a first date?

2. Have you ever been uncomfortable holding a girl's hand in public?

3. Have you ever pushed a girlfriend away who was trying to kiss you in front of your friends?

4. Have you ever slapped a girl's ass in public?

5. Ever eaten pussy on your first date?

6. Have you ever said you were gay to turn someone down who was asking you out?

7. Have you ever exaggerated to your friends about any sexual experience?

8. Have you ever had sex for more than an hour in one session?

9. Ever managed two orgasms in fewer than twenty minutes?

10. Have you ever ended up dating someone for a while who slept with you on the first date?

11. Have you ever been to a strip club?

12. A peep show?

13. A burlesque show?

14. Ever paid for a private lap dance?

15. Have you ever given a back massage with ulterior motives?

16. Would you ever give a hand job to the quarterback of your favorite team if it meant they would win the Playoffs?

17. Would you let him blow you for the Super Bowl title?

18. Ever used a women's bathroom and stayed quietly inside the stall when other people were in there who didn't know you were?

19. Did you masturbate?

20. As far as you know, has a woman ever lied to you about being pregnant with your baby?

21. Ever fucked someone while high on any drug who did not know you were?

22. Have you ever collected underwear that did not belong to you?

23. Ever reused a condom you had already used?

24. Ever used one already used by someone else?

25. Have you ever hazed anyone before letting them into a club to which you belonged?

26. Have you ever spanked or paddled anyone for nonsexual purposes?

27. How about for sexual ones?

28. Have you ever witnessed a pretty badly faked fake-orgasm?

29. Ever driven across the country by yourself without ever stopping to sleep?

30. Ever driven across three or more states on one motorcycle trip?

31. Did you learn how to play baccarat because of a James Bond movie?

32. Did you ever play an electric instrument?

33. Have you ever been to an Ozzy Osbourne concert?

34. Marilyn Manson?

35. Have you ever read *Mein Kamf*?

36. Ever read *The Communist Manifesto*?

37. Have you ever watched *The Shining*?

38. Have you ever watched *Deliverance*?

39. Do you know all the words to "Darling Nikki" by Prince?

40. Know any lyrics to any song by Crematory?

41. Have you ever been involved in a debate over which Disney princess would be the hottest fuck?

42. Was Princess Leia chained up and pressed to Jabba the Hutt ever masturbation fodder for you?

43. Did you ever hang a picture of a hot bombshell on your wall?

44. Have you ever called your girlfriend "Sugar Tits" or "Sweet Cheeks"?

45. Have you ever done so in public?

46. How about in front of her father?

47. Have you ever used duct tape to make racing stripes on your car?

48. Ever tried to clean the mud off your car with a Brillo pad?

49. Have you seen the car chase in *Bullitt* more than three times?

50. Have you ever had a wet dream?

51. The first time you came did it totally freak you out?

52. Have you ever masturbated while watching *The Blue Lagoon* starring Brooke Shields?

53. In general, has Brooke Shields ever made you want to jerk off and/or vomit?

54. Have you ever practiced using a credit card to try to jimmy a lock?

55. Practiced using a Slim Jim to open car doors?

56. Did you ever build a pyramid out of beer cans?

57. Have you ever consumed alcohol that had been poured between someone's breasts and into a cup or straight into your mouth?

58. Have you ever tried to rally your friends to break into a school?

59. Have you ever had friends tell you they could no longer hang out with you because you were starting to seem like a bad influence?

60. Has anyone's parents ever told your parents that you could no longer hang out with their child?

61. Have any parents of any of your girlfriends ever openly disapproved of you?

62. Have you ever thought about car bombing Oprah?

63. Or having sex with her?

64. Have you ever picked your nose while driving?

65. Do you jerk off more than seven times a week?

66. Are you kind of baffled why women think Sarah Jessica Parker is so cute when you are pretty sure you could do pull-ups while hanging from her nose?

67. Do you think that Charlotte, Samantha, or Miranda is hot even if you'd never admit it to anyone?

68. Or are you like, "Who the fuck are these people? Do they have big tits?"

69. Have you ever made a girl cum?

70. Ever made her cum with your tongue?

71. Have you ever let a gay guy give you head?

72. Have you ever punched your father?

73. Are you the alpha male among your friends?

74. Have you ever started a fistfight over a stolen parking spot?

75. Have you ever opted for a beer over a delicious fruity cocktail because you were in mixed company?

76. Do you have trouble drinking delicious fruity cocktails even in private?

77. Did you avoid dancing to the fast songs at high school dances?

78. Did you ever buy, borrow, or steal an instructional break-dance video?

79. Can you recite any jokes verbatim from *Eddie Murphy Raw*?

80. If you can't now, could you at one time?

81. Do you know all the words to "Baby Got Back"? Be honest!

82. Have you ever wished you lived on the Venus planet from *Star Trek*?

83. Did you just Google "Venus planet from *Star*

Trek" and totally give yourself a *yes* on the last question?

84. Have you ever tried to re-create the car jump from *The Dukes of Hazard*?

85. Have you ever stolen the Victoria's Secret catalogue out of your neighbor's mailbox?

86. Have you ever allowed yourself to be dragged to a musical (or something similar, like a Tori Amos concert) because the girl who wanted you to take her was really cute?

87. Would you ever refuse to eat mini-quiche on principle?

88. Have you ever hit on a girl at a bar only to get introduced to her very large boyfriend?

89. Ever decided, "fuck it," and continued your pursuit despite him?

90. Did you ever throw a brick through the window of the home of a girl who had broken your heart?

91. Do you prefer tits to asses?

92. Asses to tits?

93. Do you figure men who prefer "eyes" are probably gay?

94. Have you ever made a girl scream during sex?

95. Ever made one purr?

96. Did you ever try out for a school musical to meet girls?

97. Have you ever used someone else's dog or kid to pick up a lady?

98. Have you ever rolled over and fallen asleep after you came without thinking about whether your partner had cum?

99. Are you 100 percent sure you know where the clitoris is on a woman?

100. Really? Are you sure you don't want to double check?

YOUR MALE PURITY NUMBER: _____%

The Female Purity Test

Being a woman rocks (because you get to wear dresses) and sucks (because you retain more water than men). Femininity is in flux and has been throughout the ages. In some cultures, women are rulers; in others, they have to wear potato sacks over their heads. Some can wear black leather and hock loogies; others are stuck at home with a brood of whiny brats, crocheting their lives away. Ultimately, womankind's greatest achievement lies in convincing men that a woman can't work as hard when she has her period. That was a really smart one!

Look at what it means to be a woman now: Barbie is a doctor and a lot of hot ladies are detectives on TV. Women also continue to sit around in coffee shops talking about men and interpersonal relationships. Give them a romantic drama over a sports-themed comedy any day. Sure, there are also women who find gossip dull and can't get enough of the whole Ohio State/ Michigan situation and paint their homes with the team colors. There are girls who like hoop skirts and others who wear jeans. Some have long hair and others sport a buzz cut.

More than anything else, there are shoes. There are as many types of shoes as there are women. And with those shoes, women are going to walk right over this test!

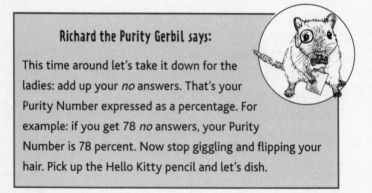

Richard the Purity Gerbil says:

This time around let's take it down for the ladies: add up your *no* answers. That's your Purity Number expressed as a percentage. For example: if you get 78 *no* answers, your Purity Number is 78 percent. Now stop giggling and flipping your hair. Pick up the Hello Kitty pencil and let's dish.

1. Ever given a blowjob on your first date in the hopes it would earn you a second?

2. Have you ever said you were a lesbian to turn someone down who was asking you out?

3. Have you ever lied to a lover about having done less with someone sexually than you actually had?

4. How about to your friends?

5. Have you ever shaved your bush into any shapes like a star or a heart or Mickey Mouse?

6. Ever had more than three orgasms in one session of sex?

7. Have you ever had sex on a first date?

8. Have you ever been to a burlesque show?

9. Ever watched an all-male revue?

10. Ever gone to a strip club with your boyfriend?

11. Ever been given a free lap dance at a strip club by a naked woman?

12. Have you ever entered the bathroom of the opposite sex while not on a rescue mission?

13. Ever farted audibly in mixed company?

14. Have you ever lied to anyone about being pregnant?

15. Ever borrowed a diaphragm?

16. Have you ever driven across the country by yourself using a blow-up of another person, a doll, or some kind of a mannequin to make it appear to your fellow travelers that you were not alone?

17. Have you ever had your upper lip waxed?

18. Have you ever frozen the bra of a sleeping person at a slumber party?

19. Ever stuck the hand of someone sleeping at a slumber party into warm water to see if they would wet the bed?

20. Ever played with a Ouija board?

21. Did you ever light candles to try to evoke spirits?

22. Ever set up candles to set the mood for seduction?

23. Have you ever called your boyfriend "Daddy"?

24. In public?

25. Ever called him "Baby Boy?"

26. How about in front of his friends?

27. Have you ever licked your lips seductively at a stranger?

28. Batted your eyes?

29. How about blown kisses?

30. Have you ever posted comments on people.com or tmz.com about reality show celebrities?

31. Did you ever think Alfalfa and Darla on *The Little Rascals* had the kind of relationship that was going to really last?

32. How about Jake Ryan and Samantha Baker from *Sixteen Candles*?

33. Did you have a crush on Judd Nelson (Bender) in *The Breakfast Club*?

34. Did you prefer Duckie over the preppy guy in *Pretty in Pink*?

35. Have you ever gone through anyone's e-mail without them knowing?

36. Have you ever chugged wine from the bottle?

37. Did you think it was weird that women were supposed to think the Fonze was hot?

38. Have you ever masturbated with water from a hose or a showerhead?

39. Have you ever met a man and decided that he should be allowed to impregnate a lot of women because of the fantastic gene pool from which he seemed to have been spawned?

40. When you were a virgin, did you believe blowjobs were a totally innocent alternative to losing your virginity?

41. Did you ever go to a hairdresser and ask for hair like Farrah Fawcett, the girls from *Facts of Life*, or Claire Danes in *My So-Called Life*?

42. Ever ask for "the Rachel"?

43. Did you ever get mad at a boyfriend for punching someone in defense of your honor?

44. In high school, were you a mean girl?

45. Have you ever farted during sex?

46. Ever queefed after?

47. Has a guy ever given you flowers on a first date and instead of thinking, "How sweet!" you knew immediately it was just never going to work?

48. Ever had to stifle a gag reflex when a boyfriend gave you chocolates and roses for Valentine's Day?

49. Did you ever cry because someone else got to play Mary in the Christmas pageant (or something similar, like Annie in the school play) and you were totally counting on it?

50. Have you ever intentionally pulled anyone's hair?

51. Did you ever go to a pop concert and cry because you couldn't contain your enthusiasm for those hot dancing boys?

52. In retrospect, does that make you want to cry?

53. Are you ready to accept that even though all girls think they are most like Carrie, we are all either Samantha or Charlotte (or, okay, Miranda if we have a biting wit and a worthwhile career)?

54. If you had to choose, would you have to go with Draco Malfoy over Ron Weasley or Harry Potter?

55. Do you think you are probably a little more like Hermione Granger than you want to accept?

56. When I say "silver earrings with a gold necklace," do you cringe?

57. When I say "penny loafers," do you think, "Making a comeback"?

58. How about shoulder pads? Are you ready to give them a crack?

59. Have you ever had a Brazilian?

60. Did you give up trying to look cool after the eleventh grade and instead begin to work with what you had?

61. Have you ever faked helplessness with a power tool to make a guy feel good about himself?

62. Have you ever faked a fear of spiders to give a man a chance to be a man?

63. Have you ever been in a relationship you had completely fought for only to find yourself desperately trying to get out?

64. Have you ever given a blowjob and thought about anything that would come to mind besides the blowjob itself just to get yourself through it?

65. Have you ever told a guy you were allergic to semen to avoid having to swallow?

66. Ever looked in a mirror and kissed your reflection?

67. Do you ever wear combat, biker, or construction worker boots with dresses?

68. Do you wear Ugg boots in the middle of summer?

69. Do you want to spit at people who do?

70. Do you sometimes think that even though you'd be a great mom, if the world is going to end in 2012, it will really suck to go through Armageddon with a toddler?

71. Do you pretty much mentally marry any decently attractive single man you've met through friends as soon as you hear that he's looking to buy property?

72. Do you mentally break up with the very same guy if instead you hear he's just had to sell his car to pay rent?

73. Did you avoid all the guys your parents would love for you to date until you were twenty-eight only to realize that those guys are in fact the only marriageable ones? But by then they were all married?

74. Inside, are you relieved you didn't marry any of the guys you have dated even though if you have to go to one more family Christmas by yourself you might blow your own brains out?

75. Have you ever read a story in the paper about some guy that killed his parents or pregnant wife and had the thought flicker in your mind, "He's kind of hot!"?

76. Have you ever written to a guy in prison to be friendly?

77. Did you get a little crush?

78. Have you ever had revenge sex with a guy?

79. Have you ever been able to not call back the guy who broke your heart when he was begging for your forgiveness?

80. Have you ever worn black eyeliner as a lip liner?

81. Did you ever wear black nail polish?

82. Have you ever worn neon pink shoes?

83. At any point in your life, did you ever own jelly shoes in more than two colors?

84. Do you have more than three wife-beater tank tops in your wardrobe?

85. Do you have any concert T-shirts that you have taken a pair of scissors to and adapted to fit your feminine frame?

86. Have you ever pretended to be a virgin because you knew the guy you wanted would prefer to think that you were?

87. Have you ever faked an orgasm?

88. Have you ever had an orgasm?

89. Have you ever had a guy ask you to stop giving him a hand job because you were hurting him?

90. How about a blowjob?

91. Have you ever gotten your tongue pierced or breast implants because some asshole asked you to?

92. Have you ever told a guy he was the best sex

you'd ever had when in fact it was like having a jackhammer tear into your nether regions?

93. Have you ever had a guy slip his penis into you only to have wondered to yourself, "Is it in?"

94. Have you ever watched TV while someone fucked you?

95. Have you ever fallen asleep while someone was fucking you?

96. Have you ever asked a guy to stop rubbing your clit because you were afraid he was going to rub it off your body?

97. Have you ever forgone an orgasm because you were feeling too tired to get there?

98. How about because your boyfriend was feeling too lazy to get you there?

99. Have you ever asked a guy to stop and taken over yourself to get off?

100. Have you ever had to show a guy where your clit was because the spot he was rubbing was in fact, in a different zip code? (If your answer is, "If I had a nickel for the number of times . . ." then go ahead and add or subtract 2 points in either direction on your final score. You deserve it!)

YOUR FEMALE PURITY NUMBER:
_____%

The Gay Purity Test

Homosexuality is such a multifaceted way of life these days. Some gays miss Reagan and others name sex juice after conservative Republican homophobes. It's hard to sum up, really. Gays in America are still as vehemently loathed by some for their rampant use of acronyms as they are loved by others for their fabulous fashion sense.

For the purposes of this test, gay purity begins by assuming that being gay is a dirty thing—in all the very best ways there are to be dirty. Then, as with all the tests in this book, it takes it even further. The questions are stereotyping, but in a good way! So buckle on those chaps, brush out your Freddie Mercury moustache, and let's get sweaty together.

Joselin Linder

Richard the Purity Gerbil says:

Hi, boys! Wipe off the mascara and let's get to work, because this test is going to be fierce. Add up your *no* answers. That's your Purity Number expressed as a percentage. For example: if you get 50 *no* answers, your Purity Number is 50 percent. Not so complicated, is it, honey? Don't be such a drama queen.

1. Are you a man that at any point in your life has shared an umbrella with another man?

2. Have you ever worn a Speedo in public and not felt ashamed?

3. Would you feel like an idiot if you found yourself muttering the phrase: "Get in there! Tackle him!" and then chugging a beer and smashing it flat against your forehead?

4. Ever given a blowjob through a glory hole?

5. Have you ever said you were straight to turn someone down for a date?

6. Have you ever made anyone straight turn bi?

7. Ever turned 'em gay? (If your answer is, "God

194

did," but they were living a straight life before they got into your bed, go ahead and give yourself a *yes*.)

8. Have you ever eaten the food used in masturbation?

9. Ever fed it to someone else?

10. Have you ever gone on a boat with five or more shirtless men and no women (unless she was employed by the company renting the boat)?

11. Have you ever been BFF with an overweight, acne-ridden yet hilarious woman who really knew how to scat or else loved old movies, and was (secretly) desperately in love with you?

12. Have you ever wished you were her?

13. Do you have a stage name?

14. Do you use your hands when you talk more than a Jewish comedian or an Italian fisherman? (Still *yes*, if you are either a Jewish comedian or an Italian fisherman.)

15. Have you ever worn chaps when you weren't on a ranch?

16. Have you ever had sex in front of an audience?

17. Have you ever had anal sex without lubrication?

18. Did you ever have sex with women?

19. Have you ever worn brown shoes with a black

belt and realized it to your horror on your lunch break?

20. In your friend group, do you have a really great, if fashionably challenged lesbian couple?

21. Did you come out of the closet within a week of realizing you were gay?

22. Did you come out of the closet even though, let's face it, you were never really in it?

23. Did you ever raid your sister's closet?

24. How about her makeup?

25. Have you ever been to a Liza Minnelli or Madonna concert?

26. Do you know who I mean when I just say "Barbra"?

27. Do you own a Chihuahua with a name that has Latin flavor?

28. Does he wear a studded collar?

29. Have you ever worn one?

30. Have you approached your sister about whether or not she'd ever consider carrying a baby for you?

31. Do you prefer bears to leathermen?

32. Leathermen to club kids?

33. Or chickens and twinks to them all?

34. Have you ever jerked off to the Brooks Brothers' catalog?

35. Ever jerked off to the L.L. Bean catalogue?

36. Ever jerked off to *Martha Stewart Living*?

37. Have you ever had a sexual fantasy about Bill Clinton?

38. How about Hillary—come on! Those pantsuits?!

39. Have you ever dressed as a minister/priest or rabbi for Halloween?

40. Have you ever dressed as a minister/priest or rabbi for sexual role-playing?

41. Have you had sexual fantasies about your father?

42. Have you had sex with your father?

43. Have you had sexual fantasies about your brother(s)?

44. Have you had sex with your brother(s)?

45. Have you ever offered a blowjob to any of your sister's boyfriends?

46. Ever had sex with her husband (your brother-in-law)?

47. Have you slept with your father-in-law?

48. Have you slept with your stepfather?

49. Have you slept with your stepbrother?

50. Have you at least had fantasies about your brother-in-law, father-in-law, stepfather, and/or stepbrother?

51. Have you ever had sex with a minister/priest or rabbi?

52. Ever jerk off to those pictures of George W. Bush in his National Guard uniform?

53. Do you find uniforms vaguely attractive?

54. Do you find fascism vaguely attractive?

55. Are you a Log Cabin Republican?

56. Does the word "log" make you snicker?

57. Does the word "Republican" make you snicker?

58. Do you wear drag when you lip-sync at home?

59. Do you wear drag when you lip-sync in public?

60. Is everything better in high heels?

61. When you fantasize about the Hardy Boys, do you pretend to be their younger brother?

62. When you fantasize about the Hardy Boys, do you pretend to be their father?

63. Have you slept with anyone from 'N Sync (in your mind)?

64. Have you slept with anyone from New Kids on the Block (in your mind)?

65. Have you slept with anyone from Backstreet Boys (in your mind)?

66. Have you slept with anyone from the Osmond family (in your mind)?

67. Have you slept with anyone from the Jackson 5 (in your mind)?

68. Have you ever "managed" a boy band?

69. Have you ever "auditioned" for a boy band?

70. Have you ever measured your penis against someone else's?

71. Do you agree with the statements: Marilyn Manson would be better in bed with his makeup?

72. And RuPaul would be better in bed without his makeup?

73. . . . but that Zac Efron can wear his makeup to bed if he wants?

74. Do you prefer to be the bottom?

75. Do you ever wish you preferred to be the bottom?

76. Or do you generally just want to watch?

77. Have you ever been in a serious relationship and pulled off having a deal with your partner that you could sleep with other guys as long as there were no last names, no trysts in your own bed, and no numbers exchanged?

78. Have you ever been in a serious relationship and went out together to pick up other guys for sex?

79. Have you ever told anyone that you went to high school with or had for a camp counselor any of the Village People?

80. Did you?

81. Have you ever gone cottaging? (Whether or not

you came across a U.S. senator while doing so is a whole other Larry Craig . . .)

82. Do you call a frothy mixture of cum and fecal matter "santorum" after the anti-gay rights senator, Rick?

83. Does your favorite movie involve a heavily made-up drunk woman crying in at least two scenes?

84. Did you ever refer to yourself as "bi-curious" in complete earnestness without a hint of amusement at either the term itself or the fact that someone came up with it?

85. Do you kick up your heels and give a *whoop whoop* to straight guys who are up for being gay-for-pay?

86. Have you done it bareback since 1985?

87. Have you ever gone cruising in a park?

88. Have you ever rimmed or been rimmed by anyone?

89. Do you believe that a butt harp is not a fictional sex toy (as some have reported) but a real-life actual sex toy, or is it that you just really want it to be true?

90. Are your nipples or tongue pierced?

91. Have you ever endured a rectal perforation?

92. Has anything traveled into your colon that you did not mean to have traveled quite so far?

93. Did you just put down this test?

94. Have you ever used any Japanese sex toys?

95. Do you own cock rings in more than one size?

96. Ever thought about getting a Prince Albert piercing?

97. Ever had your cock tattooed?

98. Have you ever participated in bondage?

99. Did you ever send a letter to anyone in a boy band declaring your love?

100. Are you feeling a little bit dirtier about yourself now that you have taken this test?

YOUR GAY PURITY NUMBER:
_____%

The Meaning Behind the Scores

0–10% Devil

11–20% Demon

21–30% Fallen Angel

31–40% Bad Boy

41–50% Bad Girl

51–60% Designated Driver

61–70% Choir Member

71–80% Angelic

81–90% Archangel

91–100% He or She Who Smells Like Mildew

Like life, Purity Numbers are fluid. Your Purity Number can and will change over time. Purity ebbs and flows over a lifetime. College, for example, offers a cornucopia of opportunities for debauchery. But if you flub that four-year opportunity and enter your twenties with an angelic score of 77 percent, all is not lost: don't hesitate to take a year to throw caution to the wind and let down your hair. But remember not to force it. Life will often throw its own impurities at you. You might not even have to try.

Meanwhile, those with Purity Numbers on the demonic end of the scale might have a rougher time improving their states of being. The truth is, once you've dropped acid in a cancer ward and slept with a monkey, the moral stains are never going to wash out. But you can always shift your perspective: if your Purity Number 1978–2009 reveals one truth about you, perhaps your Purity Number 2009–2020 will offer another, brighter truth, especially with the help of intense psychotherapy and antibiotic creams. The only thing you've really lost is a depressingly large number of brain cells.

Interpreting Your Score

1–10% Devil Let's just say it: this is pretty impure. In fact, a score in this range is a clear sign that morality and conscience have left the building, or have more than likely died squatting on the upstairs toilet in

Graceland. If you have a Purity Number this low, you almost certainly have a serious problem (not including the fact that some of your vital organs might not be in working order).

To be as serious as a heart attack, this score indicates that you are one speedball away from having an actual heart attack. If your Purity Number truly lands below 10 percent, you should reconsider your ways. Lives are in danger, principally your own. Fun can certainly be had by testing boundaries, but once you start playing hopscotch over those boundaries, you're bound to end up in diapers and a wheelchair. (For the first few months this is okay because people bring you flowers and someone gives you a sponge bath, but after a while, the flowers stop and you start to wonder if the sponge-bath water didn't come from the same bucket they used to scrub down the old guy in bed seven.)

For real excitement, focus on embracing life over cheating death. It's important to overcome your fears, but not to the point of ambivalence. Not fearing death isn't the same as not caring about life. Once you understand the distinction, you and your Purity Number can soar!

11–20% Demon If you haven't been in a rock band since 1970, you have no good excuse for a Purity Number

Richard the Purity Gerbil says:

Yo, Beelzebub! Go get yourself something to love, like a puppy, and try not to fuck it or get it stoned. Actually, maybe you should start with a goldfish and see if you can pull yourself together!

this low. It's one thing to enjoy an evening of absinthe and hashish on your European backpacking trip that ends with you paving over the cobblestones in puke. It's quite another to drink the green fairy until you end up lobbing off your own ear. But the simple fact that you're reading this is a good sign.

So give it a rest. A modicum of self-control indicates a healthy human being with the ability to connect with other human beings, and not just the alien species you run into every time you're on DMT. The greatest thing you can do when you are bending reality is to maintain clarity about what reality looks like when it is no longer bent! Interpersonal relationships are more important and fulfilling than those you might have with anime heroines or bags of Doritos.

Someday you want to be able to look back over certain periods in your life and feel a sense of pride at the

Joselin Linder

way you coexisted, served your fellow man, and treated your mother. Remember that there is an opportunity for greatness lying in every step forward.

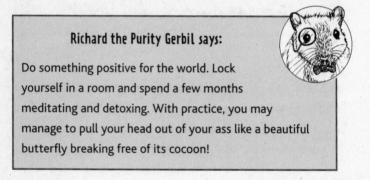

Richard the Purity Gerbil says:

Do something positive for the world. Lock yourself in a room and spend a few months meditating and detoxing. With practice, you may manage to pull your head out of your ass like a beautiful butterfly breaking free of its cocoon!

21–30% Fallen Angel It's hard to know when to start and when to stop. If you have a Purity Number in the thirtieth percentile, you've either done your share of hard living and at some point put on the breaks, or you're spiraling out of control toward a Purity Number in the teens and all the physical and emotional dangers that lie in that general direction.

Newton's first law of motion dictates that "a body in motion tends to stay in motion." Phrases like "rock bottom" and "hitting the wall" are clichés for a reason—countless recovering out-of-control-aholics vividly remember the moment they realized things had to change. Buckle up, because you're one game of underage strip poker away from the wall.

If your score falls in this range, it's time to take a little inventory. Are you sixteen years out of the navy and a guest lecturer in the Gamblers Anonymous circuit? You've probably come out the other side. However, if you spent last night doing the Backward Donkey with more or less than one other person, ask yourself if

---

Richard the Purity Gerbil says:

This must be difficult for you. On the one hand, it has been a fun life. On the other hand, you are now serving seven to twenty-five in a correctional facility outside of Tulsa. You are the girlfriend of a person called Tallulah (and you are pretty sure you are both dudes). You make Jell-O. That's what you do every day. You feel bad. You think you can do better. Others, like the pastor who visits you on Sundays and the lady writing you letters from her town (pop. 16) agree. If you stick to doing those push-ups and studying those law books, I'll be rooting for you!

---

you need an actual bottom made of rock to hit to remind you that it's okay to say no.

31–40% Bad Boy With a score in the fortieth percentile, you've probably done a lot of very bad things in your life. But someone has already whipped you for it—with leather, no less. For every whole cake you eat in one sitting, you throw in a piece of broccoli or two. For every blowjob you give or receive, you help an old blind lady get across the street without copping a feel. You think you've lived a full life. The problem is, you ain't dead yet.

If your Purity Number makes you a Bad Boy, remember that everyone wanted James Dean, but after he wrapped his Porsche around a poplar, everyone just wanted a cardboard cutout of him because the real thing was bloody and gross. So, use your sexy before you break your teeth doing another ollie. Slick back your hair, smoke your last Marlboro, and think about retiring your flask in favor of a thermos. After the guy gets the girl to throw off the poodle skirt of repression in favor of the black leather of passion come the babies. And those babies can't eat bourbon!

41–50% Bad Girl When it comes to the Purity Test, being average means you get to have a good time and

Richard the Purity Gerbil says:

The road you're on is slick with rain, twisting and turning ahead in the darkness. No need to pull over, but you're going to want to slow down and turn your headlights on. So, buckle up. And no, that is not a metaphor for virginity loss or anything to do with enemas.

actually remember it afterward. Average folks don't end up in hospitals every other weekend, or come face to face with the business end of pistols. An acid trip for you is interesting, like a science project. You sit back on the grassy knoll and simply take in the world from a new perspective. People in the fiftieth percentile don't get all crazy and start jumping off cliffs into foreign bodies of water or foreign bodies generally.

The nice thing about a score in the forties is that it indicates a semblance of control. There are just some places you people will not go. You say no to autoerotic asphyxiation and huffing gasoline. You have inhaled your share of nitrous but you thought the Mickey Mouse voice was way better than the head rush. You're the cool girl with the hoop earrings and the dark red lips.

Richard the Purity Gerbil says:

You're at a crossroads. One direction will lead you to a place where you never have to lie to your kids about the fun you had over spring break. The other involves skidmarks in your underpants. You decide.

You're the mysterious hottie who reads Kafka in the tenth grade and totally gets it.

51–60% Designated Driver You're a go-with-the-flow Joe. You drink when your friends drink. You'll be in the orgy, but only if someone else starts it and everyone involved is good-looking and reasonably clean.

If you're in the sixtieth percentile, you have the papers hidden in a drawer in case anyone ever shows up with the drugs to roll in them. You know where your roommate keeps the lighter, but yours definitely got cabbaged at the last blowout. You smoke socially, you drink for fun, and you'd never drive drunk because it's lame. You aren't what people would call a free-thinker, but you remain in control of yourself and respect your limits. That's a good thing. Stay in the fifties! The fifties suit you well!

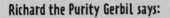

Richard the Purity Gerbil says:

You're like R.E.M.'s *Green* album. You have to respect the band even if there's nothing indie about the album.

61–70% Choir Member Right now, you're taking just enough chances to keep up. That's the way to do it. Slow and steady wins the race. Don't pressure yourself: it's okay to continue living your life at a leisurely pace. With a Purity Number in the seventieth percentile, chances are you're a good egg. You can go on the Internet without forsaking your friends and family. You can drink a glass of wine at a cocktail party and savor its nose without calculating precisely how long you'll have to wait before pouring another without pissing off your spouse.

You're feeling things out, taking your time. You're in it for the long haul. You're enjoying your life today while socking a little away for the future. Stay sensible and you'll turn out just fine—not everyone needs to go out in a blaze of glory.

> **Richard the Purity Gerbil says:**
>
> You look like a kid, either because you played it safe and stayed away from the hard stuff, or because you actually are a kid.

71–80% Angelic You're good. But not too good. You're a one-toe-in kind of guy. A stay-in-sight-of-shore kind of girl. You went to that party full of underage drinkers, but you drank Coke and pretended it had rum in it.

If this is your score, don't die of embarrassment, even if you are easily embarrassed. Life is full of opportunities. Perhaps you avoided the ones that seemed scary or painful. It would be difficult to fault you for that. Just make sure that your aversion to shoving things in places where the sun don't shine isn't an aversion to life itself.

You're lucky enough to be born in a world that has both the Internet and plastics. Something that doesn't smell good can feel fantastic. The point being, caution is well and good, but sometimes a little adventure into the unknown is stupendous. Consider doing it now because crotchless panties and octogenarians don't mix. Live a little; you've got the Purity Number to burn.

The Purity Test

> **Richard the Purity Gerbil says:**
>
> Spend too much time wondering whether that little white pill is an aspirin or someone's misplaced Xanax, and you'll just have to suffer with that headache. Take a chance and swallow.

81–90% Archangel Who's the one organizing the designated driver? You! Who's the kid with an adult who always knows where she is? You! You'd never walk down a dark road alone after midnight, even if everyone in the village was over sixty and blind. Compulsive and humorless, you take great pleasure in recreational mathematics and getting a deal on "sensible shoes." If your Purity Number is in the ninetieth percentile, chances are you haven't spent much time out of your house. But it isn't your fault. Somebody—probably the nuns who took you in when your parents abandoned you—did a very good job sheltering you from the outside world, but the fact that you're holding this book is a very good sign; you've probably lost a few points off your Purity Number just by taking the test!

So live a little. There's nothing wrong with a wholesome game of Parcheesi, a plate of cookies, and a chat

213

with your elderly landlady about her friend Sally's irritable bowel syndrome, but let this go on night after night and you will never know the simple joys of an accidental orgasm while riding a horse, or Japanese anime tentacle porn.

Richard the Purity Gerbil says:

At the rate you're going, you'll need a map if you ever decide to go looking for your asshole!

91–100% He or She Who Smells Like Mildew The sad thing is, you don't even know enough to be sad about your condition. You want for nothing because you have no idea what it is you're supposed to want. People think you dress funny because you were home-schooled on a "compound," but really it's because you are blind and deaf to the world around you.

Yes, it's true anyone can get hit by a car, have a broken heart, trip into a meat grinder, or get kidnapped. It's a dangerous world and you're vulnerable. But you could fall in love, learn to sing, buy a very cool bike that everyone wants, or wear a turquoise leotard! What do you have to lose? Take a strand of your six-foot-long beard and use it as a bookmark for your Penguin Classic. If you get up, step over the piles of newspapers, and go toward the light, you just might discover a world worth exploring and a life worth living. If not, you can always go back to your book—that is, if that meat grinder didn't get you!

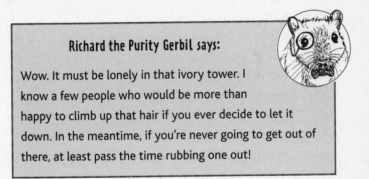

Richard the Purity Gerbil says:

Wow. It must be lonely in that ivory tower. I know a few people who would be more than happy to climb up that hair if you ever decide to let it down. In the meantime, if you're never going to get out of there, at least pass the time rubbing one out!

"Celebrity" Results

Are you curious how your score fares relative to the scores of celebrities, fake-celebrities, people who wish they were celebrities, and complete nobodies? Read on and see how the mighty are scoring and offer up your own testimonial to see how you compare! (Last names have been abbreviated or dropped to protect absolutely no one and nothing.)

Ricki, graduate student and 84% pure:
So apparently there are a LOT of ways to be impure . . . and I am, pretty much, none of them. I found myself a little bit cheating to be more impure . . . That's bad, right? I do feel like a bit of a prude . . . though to be honest, I am a bit of a prude.

Ryan, rock star and 52% pure:
I can't decide if that score is something to be proud of or ashamed of. I'm a little of both.

Gabe, entrepeneur and 64% pure:
:)

Martin, Scottish person and 55% pure:
If I was cocaine I would be shite. If I was a priest I'd be dodgy. If I was chocolate I would be rubbish. If I was a diamond I'd be cheap. If I was a dog I'd be a mongrel. If I was honest I'd be a liar!

Kevin, teacher and 40% pure:
I haven't been pure since the mid-'80s.

Gregory, actor and 61% pure:
Um, the test made me feel very exposed, and a little sad, actually.

Nadia, lawyer and 58% pure:
At least no one asked if I'd ever slept with a televange-list.

Alina, singer and 86% pure:
You know, taking the test brings up a lot of interest-ing memories and occasional internal conflicts as one tries to navigate the gray areas of purity. Like, maybe you didn't steal money from the place you worked, but you steal tampons, so how pure are you? But is steal-ing tampons really bad? Does your purity in this case depend on what you stole and why? I have to admit that one question made me remember that I HAD once called out someone else's name in the midst of . . . um, you know . . . and after I apologized endlessly, he said, "That's okay, Jennifer." (My name's not Jennifer.)

Amanda, graphic designer and 72% pure:
I think I am pretty comfortable with my score. I am a poseur anyway. I like to act like I'm more mischievous or have a history/reputation when I really do not. For example, I carry around a helmet as if I ride a motor-cycle when really all I've got is a scooter. I'm that kind of girl. That's who I am, and honestly, the older I get, the more comfortable I am accepting that I'm just a simple scooter rider.

Stephanie, actor/artistic director and 87% pure:
Frankly, I am a little shocked by some of what I read—

Gabra, actress and 59% pure:
Certain things shocked me, like the immediate yes answer in my head to "Do you like the taste of semen?" I went back and questioned that, but since the yes seemed to come instinctively (no pun intended), I went with it.

Sean, operations manager and 56% pure:
How do I feel about this test? Know that I am now actively searching for an Amish bartender who is a patient at a hospital so I can put on a nice short dress and stilettos with which I will fuck the shit of out her cheek dimples.

Patrick, taxman and 34% pure:
I'd like to clear it up that I was never technically "fired" for sucking nitrous, but I'll admit I was officially written up for it when I worked at Ritzy's when I was fifteen.

Mary, freelance writer and 95% pure:
I think I may need to get out more . . .

The Purity Test

Erin, photographer and 85% pure:
A lot of things have now come to my attention that I should try to make life a little more interesting!

Stan, professional juror and 17% pure:
Most of the test seemed straightforward, but I guess I had some follow-up questions on a few items which may affect my score:

- *Would calling your lover "Big Mamma" count as a yes?*
- *Regarding insertion of fruits/vegetables—do tubers/starches count? (spirit of the law?)*
- *What if I watched a porn where a person is dressed as animal excrement?*
- *What do you mean by "ice cream cone"?*

Purity Reference Guide

For Those with Low Scores

STD Testing Centers

www.requestatest.com
A Web site that will lead you to dependable STD
testing centers nationwide.

Suicide Prevention Hotline

1-800-273-TALK (Suicide Prevention Resource Center)

Addiction Resources

New York
St. Jude Retreat House
12 Chestnut St.
Amsterdam, NY 12010

California
Beacon House
P.O. Box 301
Pacific Grove, CA 93950

Wyoming
Cedar Mountain Treatment Center
707 Sheridan Avenue
Cody, Wyoming 82414

Quitting Smoking Resources

An effective herbal supplement that comes with a
useless-but-funny-to-sample (if you're a DJ) CD of
inspirational speaking can be found at: www
.smokeaway.com.

A Million Little Pieces by James Frey, the guy who
pissed off Oprah with the nonmemoir. It has some
great tips for quitting addicts. Read that in tandem
with *Dry* by Augusten Burroughs and anything else
you can find by reformed addicts as you quit.

Join a Web site like www.quitnet.com because you can
go to chat rooms with other weirdos quitting and
expel some of the inevitable rage you will have over
the Internet.

Don't use patches or gum. Just quit. What are you? A man or a baby? Or a babyman?

Alcoholics Anonymous Contact Info

A.A. World Services, Inc.
P.O. Box 459
New York, NY 10163
Tel: (212) 870-3400
http://www.alcoholics-anonymous.org

Al-Anon
1-800-4AL-ANON
http://www.al-anon.alateen.org/

Narcotics Anonymous Contact Info

NA World Services, Inc.
PO Box 9999
Van Nuys, CA 91409
Tel: (818) 773-9999
http://www.na.org

American Psychological Association (APA)

You can obtain a referral to a psychologist in your area by calling:
1-800-964-2000
www.apa.org

For Those with High Scores

Dating Mixers

Speed dating and Mix and Mingle parties nationwide
are sponsored by:
www.fastlife.com

Online Dating Services

Religious wackjobs use eHarmony:
www.eharmony.com

Import a Russian bride at: www.chanceforlove.com

If you are interested in slutty folks, try Nerve:
www.nerve.com

For desperate girls with oral fixations and dorky guys
with bank accounts try: www.jdate.com

Women's Sexuality and Information Centers

Center for Young Women's Heath:
http://www.youngwomenshealth.org/sexuality_menu
.html
Planned Parenthood:
www.plannedparenthood.com

Lingerie stores and online shopping

Frederick's of Hollywood
To request a catalogue (to order from or jerk off to) call:
1-800-323-9525
www.fredericks.com

Victoria's Secret
To request a catalogue (to order from or jerk off to) call:
1-800-411-5116
www.victoriassecret.com

Recommended Reading

Justine by the Marquis de Sade
Delta of Venus by Anaïs Nin
Kama Sutra by Vatsyayana
Exit to Eden by Anne Rice
Tropic of Cancer by Henry Miller